"Reading this book feels just like you are sitting on a sofa in sweatpants crisscross from besties who know exactly what you're going through because they've been there too. Each page is a gift, filled with heart-to-heart encouragement, wisdom and creativity for finding joy and faith in every season!"

MELISSA MICHAELS

New York Times best-selling author of *Love the Home You Have*, *The Inspired Room*, *Make Room for What You Love,* and *The Inspired Room Coloring Book*

"If you are ever in need of a little encouragement or inspiration, *Life in Season* is the book for you. Chapter after chapter and page after page are full of beautiful photos and inspirational projects. But what truly spoke to me about the book was that Heather's and Vanessa's hearts are written into every line. *Life in Season* is truly a treat for the soul."

KARIANNE WOOD

creator of Thistlewood Farms

"The book *Life in Season* is as beautiful on the inside as it is on the outside. This book is inviting, captivating, and refreshing. I can see why the title of this book is *Life in Season*, as it draws you in, bringing you hope for whatever season of life you are currently in."

KATIE FARRELL

author of the *Dashing Dish Cookbook* and the *Dashing Dish Devotional*

"For a non-DIYer like myself, Heather and Vanessa are a breath of fresh air. Their compelling combination of inspiration and imagination make handmade and home-made creativity possible. They turn my "I can't" into "I can" with every idea they share."

GLYNNIS WHITWER

author of *Taming the To Do List*, Executive Director of Communications at Proverbs 31 Ministries

"It's a whole new perspective on DIY! This book adds a fresh layer to the art of creating a lovely home and welcoming friends. Not only will you find some great, doable ideas, but you'll find encouragement and life-giving lessons through each project. I picked it up thinking it would inspire me to improve my home and hostess skills and put it down feeling grateful for the woman God has created me to be. It's a great read for anyone wanting to improve their home and their heart."

LISA PENNINGTON

author of *Mama Needs a Do-Over: Simple Steps for Turning a Hard Day Around*,

creator of The Pennington Point

LIFE IN
Season

CELEBRATE THE MOMENTS
THAT FILL YOUR HEART & HOME

VANESSA HUNT &
HEATHER PATTERSON

Authors of At the Picket Fence Blog

Library of Congress Control Number: 2016941914

For foreign and subsidiary rights, contact rights@worthypublishing.com

ISBN: 978-1-61795-678-2

Cover Deisgn: Melissa Reagan
Interior Layout: Bart Dawson
Cover Image: Adobe Marketplace
Photos by shutterstock.com and Vanessa Hunt and Heather Patterson
All Project Photos by Vanessa Hunt and Heather Patterson
Author photos © Valerie Hibler Photography

Printed in China
20 19 18 17 16 RRD 8 7 6 5 4 3 2 1

TO EVERYTHING
THERE IS A SEASON, AND A TIME
FOR EVERY PURPOSE UNDER HEAVEN.

Ecclesiastes 3:1 NKJV

· ·

*W*e would like to dedicate this book to our parents, Michael and Carol, who wove a love of words into the very fiber of our beings, you were the first storytellers in our lives. You might not have been able to help us much with math, but we freely give you credit for all of those A's we received in our English and language classes. You will always be our very first editors. You are both incredibly gifted writers and we share this dream come true with you. Most importantly, we are forever grateful for the solid foundation you gave us of faith in Jesus Christ and the example of what it looks like to live for Him and love others with His love. Your constant support and encouragement have carried us through all of life's seasons and we are so very thankful that you are not only our parents but our friends as well. We love you both so much and promise to get you those T-shirts made with our faces on them as requested.

We would also like to dedicate this book to our grandmothers, Opal Reddin and Beryl Kaiser-Underwood. One a professor, one a farmer's wife, both lovers of the written word, but more importantly, both women who loved the Lord and followed Him until their very last breath here on earth. The legacy they left behind will make an impact for generations to come.

· ·

CONTENTS

Summer

Autumn

Winter

INTRODUCTION

· ·

*I*n 2010, two sisters began dreaming of a community. They imagined women walking out of their front doors and meeting neighbors and friends where their fences intersected. They would talk over the pickets, drink coffee, swap recipes, share a great home décor idea or two, and invest in each other's lives. This community would be where they could laugh together over their child's latest antics and cry together over the difficult things in life. This community would be where they could talk about God and His plan for them.

We wanted to create a community that wouldn't be limited by geography. It would be available to women each day no matter where they lived. We began meeting them online At the Picket Fence. We shared our recipes and our crafts and our hearts and our faith.

And you came. You met us there at the fence and you continue to meet us there all of these years later. So, this book is dedicated to you—our dear readers, our community, our friends.

Spring

Spring is the time of year filled with new growth, when the world seems to be awakening and stretching its arms out to embrace a fresh start. Spring is also the time for planting and looking forward to the days when we will see the fruits of our labor. It's a time of hope and expectancy.

In our faith, we get to experience God's love in fresh new ways in spring. It's a time for renewal, and brings with it opportunities for growth. We are reminded every year in this season of the great sacrifice of our Lord and Savior, Jesus Christ, and the miracle of His resurrection.

A LIFE UNFOLDED

· ·

When I was in high school, I worked at the clothing store Express. As it was considered the new, trendier, sister store of The Limited, I felt like I had scored big-time, and I kept a running list of all the things I was going to buy with my employee discount. Anyone who has worked in retail clothing will tell you that it all sounds like fun and games until you find yourself elbow-deep in boxes of clothes, all waiting to be ironed and properly displayed, and you have to deal with grumpy customers while you attempt to figure out how to work the register. Probably the most essential tool for the clothing retail employee is the folding board. It looks like a clipboard without the clip part and is used to get those shirts folded like little soldiers all in a row on the display shelves. I loved this tool! It spoke right to my neat-freak heart and I got such a sense of satisfaction out of using it to get the perfect fold. And then the inevitable would happen. Some customer would have the nerve to come along and dig through those perfectly folded shirts to find the size they needed, leaving my precise little soldiers all rumpled and wrinkled and a shell of their former, perfectly folded selves.

I don't know about you, but throughout my life, when I heard the word *unfolded*, it always conjured up images of a soft and flowing process. You hear someone reference the "unfolding" of a story and you envision something almost magical, holding your breath as each new chapter reveals itself. I'm always particularly reminded of this in the spring as we watch and wait for the moment when new life emerges on the branches, a bud unfolding to reveal the blossom inside. But think about what must happen for that bud to appear. There's pushing and straining in order for it to finally break through the surface of the branch. I think the reality is that most of the time, the process of unfolding something isn't quite so magical. It's rumpled, it's wrinkled, it's messy, and it's anything but perfect.

> Perhaps, it's only in the painful situations that strip us bare and take us to a place where we can actually see ourselves in all of our imperfect glory.

For most of my life, I tried very hard to stay folded up. I wanted my life to look like those crisp shirts, stacked up all neat and tidy on the display shelves. But God had other plans for me. My life became unfolded.

I thought that if I did everything just perfectly and made all the right choices, I could sail through life with barely a wrinkle. It wasn't that I thought I would never face challenges, but I assumed that I could avoid most of them through sheer determination.

After I married the love of my life, we discovered that having children would be a very difficult thing for us. And with that discovery, I realized just how much in life is truly outside my control. You might think that this is the time when everything became unfolded. You would be wrong. Because, you see, this was really only the moment when my folded-up life was removed from the shelf. The unfolding began when, despite my pain and grief, I welcomed the unique opportunity that the Lord was giving me: the opportunity

to peel back the layers of my heart. And as each layer was peeled away, I was startled by what was revealed. I discovered that I was a rumpled, wrinkled, imperfect mess.

What I wanted was simply to be comforted in my hurt. I just wanted God to wrap me up in His peace. And He did give me that. In the moments when I felt like I couldn't breathe because the pain was just too great, I understood what Psalm 147:3 really means when it says, "He heals the brokenhearted and binds up their wounds." But I also realized that, sometimes, in our most painful moments He is calling us to something else as well. He's calling us to take a closer look at the sin in our lives. And perhaps, it's only the painful situations that strip us bare and take us to a place where we can actually see ourselves in all of our imperfect glory.

Endure hardship as discipline; God is treating you as his children. For what children are not disciplined by their father? If you are not disciplined—and everyone undergoes discipline—then you are not legitimate, not true sons and daughters at all. Moreover, we have all had human fathers who disciplined us and we respected them for it. How much more should we submit to the Father of spirits and live! They disciplined us for a little while as they thought best; but God disciplines us for our good, in order that we may share in his holiness. No discipline seems pleasant

at the time, but painful. Later on, however, it produces a harvest of
righteousness and peace for those who have been trained by it. (Hebrews
12:7–11)

When we are willing to look at hardship—at our life unfolding—as discipline, it changes everything. Or at least, it should. We should see it as an opportunity. It's an opportunity to see ourselves in a new way, to see ourselves the way God sees us. By realizing my hardships are actually a way that I can draw closer to my heavenly Father and be changed to reflect His heart, I can see them in a different light.

Are you ready to start seeing the beauty in living a life unfolded? Because where you look down and see a wrinkly, rumpled, imperfect mess, God looks down and sees that you are at *exactly* the right place for an amazing journey to begin. A journey that will be painful. A journey that will leave you untidy, undone, and unfolded. But I can guarantee that you will not be left unchanged.

We think everything looks cuter in a mason jar, and these bird's nest cupcakes are no exception.

BIRD'S NEST CUPCAKES IN MASON JARS

INGREDIENTS

- (1 8.25-oz.) package white cake mix
- 3 egg whites
- 1¼ cups buttermilk
- 2 Tbs. vegetable oil
- 1 tsp. lemon extract
- 1 (16-oz.) jar apricot-pineapple preserves
- ½ cup lemon curd
- 1 (16-oz.) container cream cheese frosting
- 1 (6-oz.) package flaked coconut
- Hershey candy-coated eggs, blue
- ½ pint mason jars

INSTRUCTIONS

Preheat oven to 350° F.

Beat first 5 ingredients at low speed with an electric mixer 30 seconds or just until moistened; beat at medium speed 2 minutes. Pour batter into cupcake liners in muffin pans. Will make approximately 24 cupcakes.

Bake for 16–18 minutes. Cupcakes are done when center springs back. Do not overbake.

Allow to cool on wire rack.

While cupcakes are cooling, spread coconut in even layer on cookie sheet or baking pan and toast at 350° F for about 10 minutes until light brown. Stir occasionally while toasting. Allow to cool.

LAYERING INSTRUCTIONS

Place one cupcake upside down in each mason jar. Top with a tablespoon of lemon curd and spread to cover cupcake. Pipe frosting to cover lemon curd. Top with tablespoon of toasted coconut.

Add another cupcake right-side up. Top with a tablespoon of preserves and spread to cover. Pipe frosting on top to cover completely and form a slight mound. Press in toasted coconut to make "nest" using thumb to gently make an indentation. Place three candy eggs in middle.

Repeat for each jar. Will make approximately 8 servings.

CLEAN FAUCETS
& CLEAN HEARTS

• •

J stood in front of the bathroom mirror one morning, moaning and groaning over the fine lines and wrinkles that had suddenly decided to make their appearance. On a day when I was already feeling impatient and discouraged, this did not help to improve my mood. It seemed like one day my skin was smooth and supple and the next day I woke up to a road map running across my face. As I was pondering what miracle cream I should purchase the next time I was at the store, I glanced down at the sink and saw it. I had to look a little closer to make sure my eyes weren't deceiving me, but sure enough, there it was—a ring of grime around the faucet. Honestly! All the kids had been asked to do was clean the bathroom. The beautiful sunshine streaming in the window on that spring day only emphasized just how poorly they had done this seemingly simple task. It also emphasized my wrinkles, but that was beside the point. Is it too much to expect teenagers to put a little bit of effort into their chores? Apparently it is.

On a morning when I was already feeling critical of myself, it wasn't much of a stretch to become very critical of my children. Before I knew it, I was hollering down the hall at them. "Am I the only one around here who can clean the bathroom well? Does no one know what it means to actually scrub the sink? Did you even have your eyes open while you were cleaning?"

I worked up such a strong dose of what I believed was completely justified indignation that I was determined to march them into that bathroom and show them just how horrible of a job they had done. I needed them to see the dirt they'd missed. I needed to point out that ring of grime around the faucet so that not only would they really understand my anger but they also would be sufficiently chastised into never doing it again.

But as I marched down the hallway toward their bedrooms I could hear God's voice whispering to me. He called me to stop, to look more closely at my own heart in that moment. And what I saw there was far worse than the wrinkles I had spotted on my face just moments earlier. I saw a ring of dirt and grime and blackness around my heart that gave the sink a run for its money. I was instantly convicted, and felt so ashamed of my quick temper and the desire to see the worst in my children. Grime around a bathroom faucet isn't really harmful, but the grime around my heart most definitely is. It's the grime that drives me to be so quick to criticize the very people I love the most. It causes me to lash out in anger and frustration instead of acting with love and gentleness. It causes me to focus on all their

> In order for me to show grace to those around me, I not only have to be aware of my own need for it, but I also have to be willing to let go of my expecations of others.

flaws when mine are so much more obvious. Or at least they should be more obvious.

> *How can you say to your brother, 'Brother, let me take out the speck that is in your eye,' when you yourself do not see the log that is in your own eye? You hypocrite, first take the log out of your own eye, and then you will see clearly to take out the speck that is in your brother's eye. (Luke 6:42 NASB)*

Isn't it always so much easier to spot someone else's grime? Our sinful nature tends to get great pleasure out of finding fault with others. It's as though by seeing their flaws we are distracted from seeing our own. On that day, my desire to point out exactly how my children had failed was very tempting. But how can I not extend them grace when my heavenly Father extends it to me over and over? Author and inspirational speaker Emily Freeman says, "Showing grace means releasing someone of the responsibility to meet my needs." In order for me to show grace to those around me, I not only have to be aware of my own need for it, but I also have to be willing to let go of my expectations of others. Does this mean I excuse my children's behavior or never reprimand them for disobeying? Of course not. But it does mean that I have to approach them differently. I have to do what God does for me. Hope for obedience, but offer a heavy dose of mercy and forgiveness when they don't do as I've expected. My job isn't to be a spirit breaker; it's to be a spirit restorer. And that definitely won't be accomplished by hollering about their lack of cleaning abilities.

> *Behold, you delight in truth in the inward be-ing, and you teach me wisdom in the secret heart. Purge me with hyssop, and I shall be*

clean; wash me, and I shall be whiter than snow. Let me hear joy and gladness; let the bones that you have broken rejoice. Hide your face from my sins, and blot out all my iniquities. Create in me a clean heart, O God, and renew a right spirit within me. (Psalm 51:6–10 ESV)

Soon I could feel God righting my spirit. I quietly made my way back into the bathroom. I looked down at the sink again and realized that it wasn't actually as dirty as I thought it was. In fact, the bathroom was fairly neat and clean. The kids really had done a pretty good job. I turned off the light and went to thank them for cleaning the bathroom.

PATINA

There are several pieces of furniture in my home that I consider heirlooms. They have been passed down from generation to generation and moved across the country and back again. They are part of so many of my childhood memories that they practically feel like members of our family. My daughter sleeps on the same bed that my mom slept in when she was a little girl, with the matching dresser nearby. Those same pieces were in my sister's room many years ago and we spent countless hours on that big oak bed pretending that it was our wagon as we reenacted our favorite *Little House on the Prairie* episodes.

The dresser was used as a changing table for both of my babies. It wasn't until it was moved into my son's nursery that I noticed something odd about the attached mirror: There were areas where it looked cloudy and discolored. I asked my mom about it and she told me a story that made these particular heirlooms even more precious to me.

My mom grew up on a farm in Michigan. When I was a little girl I absolutely loved hearing her tell stories about her childhood. She would recount the time when she and her best friend were determined to sleep in the barn one night, only to be frightened out of their wits by her older brother, who couldn't resist tormenting his little sister. Or she would tell us about attending a one-room country schoolhouse with her aunt as the teacher, and how she loved having her very own cow. But in all those years of stories, somehow the story of the fire was never part of her repertoire.

When my mom was sixteen years old, she arrived home one day after working her shift as a carhop at the A&W, to find the road to their farmhouse completely blocked off by fire trucks. She ran toward the house and saw firemen shoveling burned debris, water, and her belongings out of her bedroom window. She vividly remembers seeing the charred remains of her favorite doll lying in the yard. The fire, caused by faulty wiring, had started in the attic, above my mom's bedroom. Thankfully, it didn't spread further than that, but the damage, both emotionally and physically, was still significant. The oak bed and dresser in my daughter's room survived that fire, but the clouded mirror would always bear testimony to the event.

> The patina on my relationship with God is a reflection of what has been produced through my times of suffering.

These days, vintage furniture is all the rage—the more chipped, distressed, and antiqued the better! I love seeing the reminders of family history in those heirloom pieces of furniture in my home: the nicks and scratches, the watermarks and places where the finish has worn off. Everywhere is the evidence of years of wear and tear. We look at those pieces and we lovingly declare them to have "character."

In my backyard I have a potting bench and on that bench is evidence of my forgetfulness. Every year as the cold weather approaches I manage to remember to dump out my potted plants, but in my hurry I've been known to leave my clay pots sitting out all winter long. And when I return in the spring, ready to plant again, those  clay pots definitely look different. They have a new patina. But, for the same reasons I love my antique furniture, I really love the look of the patina on my clay pots. I like the nuances of color and texture. I like it so much that sometimes I've even taken new clay pots and painted them to look aged. To look like they have patina.

But while I'm more than happy to celebrate the patina on furniture or clay pots, sometimes I'm more hesitant to embrace the patina on my heart. Instead of seeing the wear and tear that has come through the challenges I've faced in my life as beautiful, I regard it as blemished.

Romans 5:3–5 says, "Not only so, but we also glory in our sufferings, because we know that suffering produces perseverance; perseverance, character; and character, hope." In order for those clay pots to have developed patina by the time I see them again in the spring, they must have gone through quite a weatherization. They had to experience some suffering to get all of that beautiful character. And I think that it is time for me to start celebrating my own patina, to choose to look at all of my nicks and scratches as a necessary part of my faith journey and the evidence of just how far I've come.

The process of something obtaining patina is one that is layered and produced by exposure to the elements. Similarly, the patina on my relationship with God is a reflection of what has been produced through my times of suffering. There is a layer that shows how the challenges have created a kind of perseverance in me I never knew I was capable of. And that perseverance keeps me moving forward in the face of adversity. This then produces the next layer, which is character. It's through persevering that my character is developed and strengthened in such a way that I begin to reflect the character of my heavenly Father. And it's only after perseverance and character that we reach the final layer, the one that is the most visible. One would think that hope would come first, but in the passage from Romans we see that hope comes as a product of perseverance and character. Having been through suffering, through the wear and tear and weatherization of life, hope is what shines through in the end. And with hope as the layer that everyone sees, we are proudly declaring that we embrace our patina. We celebrate those nicks and scratches and treasure them just as much as we treasure our heirlooms.

The sweetness of spring
is captured in this simple
tabletop craft. Get your
little helpers to join in
the fun of creating with
this easy project.

EASTER EGG
TABLETOP DÉCOR

SUPPLIES

_ wood spools
  (*found at craft stores*)
_ plastic or wooden
  Easter eggs
  (*colors of your choice*)
_ moss
_ marker
_ hot glue gun

INSTRUCTIONS

1 Paint the wood spools or leave unfinished if you prefer.

2 Attach a small amount of moss to the top of each spool using hot glue.

3 Using your marker, spell out the word "Easter" on the eggs, assigning each letter to a different egg.

4 Using hot glue, attach the egg to the top of the moss and hold in place, gently pressing down for a few seconds until it is stable and secure.

THE IN-BETWEEN

· ·

I remember the day it hit me: *This* was my life now. I think, if I remember correctly, I was putting yet another load of laundry in the washing machine while jiggling a whimpering, teething baby on my hip with my phone tucked under my chin while on hold to speak with a nameless, faceless operator at some call center located in another country. I say I "think" I remember, because at that time in my life I felt like that load of laundry. Wash, rinse, dry, and repeat. Wake up, drink coffee, kiss husband good-bye, wipe runny noses, pick up toys, wash clothes, pay bills, make dinner, put kids in their beds, fall into my bed, and repeat. I felt like I was in a desolate, lonely place. A wilderness of monotony, wandering in circles. Have you ever been lost in the woods? Like, really lost? There's that moment when you realize you've passed the same tree with the broken branch twice now and you are right back where you started and have to repeat the process over again, hoping this time to find a new path that takes you out of the woods.

I'm not a big fan of the in-between seasons. And I'm reminded of this each year when the world around me is trying to decide whether it's ready to move into the next season. The calendar might have declared that it is spring, but the weather forecast calls for snow. And we get frustrated and anxious as we wait for the climate to catch up to the calendar.

I often think about the lives of the Israelites when they were living in the wilderness and wonder what it must have been like to wander around in the same barren land year after year after year. Forty of them, to be exact.

Not one of you will enter the land I swore with uplifted hand to make your home, except Caleb son of Jephunneh and Joshua son of Nun. As for your children that you said would be taken as plunder, I will bring them in to enjoy the land you have rejected. But as for you, your bodies will fall in this wilderness. Your children will be shepherds here for forty years, suffering for your unfaithfulness, until the last of your bodies lies in the wilderness. For forty years—one year for each of the forty days you explored the land—you will suffer for your sins and know what it is like to have me against you. (Numbers 14:30–34)

We know that they were in the wilderness as a punishment, and that most of them would never even get to see the Promised Land. Can you

imagine how they felt? So defeated and so lost. They may have even believed that it was better to just give up. And yet, we know that they didn't. Most went on to live a whole lifetime in that wilderness. Can you imagine that for a minute? A whole lifetime. A lifetime of births and marriages. Of celebrations and funerals. Children were born every day into the wandering, born and raised in the wilderness, in this in-between place. I like to think that, while this place was temporary, and let's be honest, painful for the Israelites, it's also a place where a lot of living happened.

This is often a challenge for us as Christians, as women, as wives and moms. We often find that many of the years of our lives feel like the in-between places. We start to feel stuck and then resentful and then resigned. We forget to actually live in the in-between. If I was honest with myself, I have to admit as a wife, stay-at-home mom, and homeschooler, much of my life has felt like I've lived it in the in-between. I find myself saying, "Just wait. Wait until the kids are grown and gone, until I can have my own career and life, until my husband retires, until we can travel and have fun and really live our lives." I find myself becoming resentful

> I go through the motions of living but forget to actually live, to live right there in that moment.

of being in this place, my personal wilderness. I let myself become dry and parched. In my resentment, I go through the motions of living but forget to actually live, to live right there in that moment. I forget to stop and find the beauty around me in the everyday. I stop seeking water, I thirst for something more, but forget where to find the source to satisfy my thirst, the Living Water that always quenches.

How often have we had our mothers, or aunts, or mentors in our lives say, "Enjoy these days because they go by so fast," and we grimace and nod, all the while thinking that they must have forgotten how hard this season is and what it's like to feel so stuck, so tired, so stagnant. Yet we know they are right. The saying, "The days are long but the years are short," is so true. Even in their sinfulness and disobedience, even when they were wandering in the wilderness, God did not abandon the Israelites. He provided for their needs. And it's the same for me and for you. Take time to drink from the refreshing Living Waters that are provided to us daily. Get into the manna of His Word! God is with you and cares about each moment of your life, even the ones spent doing laundry and paying bills, and wiping bottoms and noses. Embrace this "in-between" season. Take hold of His promise to see you through every season of your life. The desert seasons of life will come and go, but the moments found in them and created in them will be your legacy . . . your promised land!

THE WORRY JAR

• •

*L*ook what I made today in Sunday school, Mommy!" My daughter excitedly ran toward me as we stood in the church lobby. She stretched out her little hand to reveal her latest creation and said, "It's a worry jar and I want you to have it." I peered down at the tiny jar with tissue paper glued all over it and did all of the appropriate oohing and aahing before replying, "Thank you so much, sweetie, I just love it!" As I turned to show it off to the rest of the family, I said to myself, "I think I'm going to need a bigger worry jar than this!"

You see, for most of my life worrying has been akin to breathing for me. My husband used to say that if I could get paid to worry we would be millionaires! And, unfortunately, my children have picked up on this particular struggle in my life. So much so that I'm pretty sure my daughter knew I needed this worry jar more than she did.

When we got home from church, my sweet girl went right into our room and placed the worry jar on my nightstand. "So you'll see it every day, Mommy," she said. And I did. I saw it every day. For the first few days I couldn't stop myself from feeling that it was almost mocking me. Reminding me that all my worries, my fears, and my concerns would never fit within its small space.

What about my deep, almost paralyzing, fear that something would happen to my husband or my children? That's way too big for such a tiny jar! What about that fractured relationship that seems so far beyond repair? It needs twenty jars! What about those moments when I'm almost certain I am falling short in my role as a mom? That needs an entire worry room—not just a jar! One day I walked into the bedroom and I noticed that the worry jar had been filled with some of the rose petals my daughter had collected off the ground during our walk. After being cooped up all winter, we were embracing the beautiful spring days. I said loudly, "Now, I wonder how on earth these rose petals got here!" And she came into the room, grinning from ear to ear. "I thought your jar needed filling up, Mommy," she said.

> Do not be anxious about anything, but in every situation, by prayer and petition, with thanksgiving, present your requests to God. And the peace of God, which transcends all understanding, will guard your hearts and your minds in Christ Jesus.
>
> Philippians 4:6–7

But I knew the truth. My jar was already filled up. In fact, it was overflowing with worry. Worry had become my way of thinking that somehow I had control over everything in my life. And this false sense of control meant that I didn't need to turn to the One who really is in control.

As my daughter left the room, I noticed she had turned the jar around. You see, that tissue paper was only glued to one side. The other side had a little scrap of paper, lovingly cut out by little six-year-old fingers. I read the words written on that scrap of paper, intended to be part of a Sunday school lesson for first graders, as though I was reading them for the very first time. In that moment, I realized the truth about my worry jar. It doesn't need to be any bigger. In fact, I don't need one at all. This is the message on the other side of the jar:

Therefore I tell you, do not worry about your life, what you will eat or drink; or about your body, what you will wear. Is not life more than food, and the body more than clothes? Look at the birds of the air; they do not sow or reap or store away in barns, and yet your heavenly Father feeds them. Are you not much more valuable than they? Can any one of you by worrying add a single hour to your life? (Matthew 6:25–27)

And the answer is no. No, I can't add an hour to my life by worrying. No, I can't protect my family from everything bad in the world. No, I can't fix that fractured relationship all on my own. No, I can't let my fear that I'm not being the best mom in the whole world paralyze me in my parenting. But what I can do is put my trust and my hope in the One who not only made the heavens and the earth but also knows the number of hairs on my head. Does putting my trust in Him mean that nothing bad will ever happen or that all of my relationships will be perfect or that I will seem like the mother of the year to all of my friends and family? Of course not. What it does mean is that He will always be with me. He'll be with me in the glorious mountain-top moments of my life, and He'll be with me in the painful valley moments.

And what about my worry jar? Well, just because I realized I don't really need it doesn't mean I won't keep it. After all, it was given to me by my favorite girl in the whole world. I still keep it on my nightstand. But now I see a jar with no lid to hold in those worries while they swirl and simmer. Now I see freedom.

New clay pots made to
look old and weathered
might be the only time
we support the speeding
up of the aging process.

FAUX-AGED CLAY POTS

SUPPLIES

_ clay pot
_ 3 foam brushes
_ paper towels
_ bowl of water
_ craft paint in white
_ blue and green colors
(*use outdoor craft paint if you are planning on keeping these pots outside*)

INSTRUCTIONS

1. Using a foam brush, lightly cover the entire clay pot in white paint. Allow to dry for about one minute.

2. Take a paper towel, dampen it with water, and then begin rubbing it on the clay pot to remove some of the paint here and there.

3. Work your way around the pot until you have the look you desire. Allow it to completely dry.

4. Once dry, repeat the process with the blue and green paints.

5. For a more authentic look, go a bit heavier with the blue and green paint around the rim and the bottom of the pot, where patina would naturally build if exposed to the elements, and don't wipe too much of those colors off in that area.

6. Allow to dry and enjoy with your favorite plants or herbs.

CERTAINTY IN THE UNKNOWN

• •

There's nothing scarier for a car owner. You're traveling down the road and you hear an ambiguous noise. You know the one. The noise that happens intermittently as you're driving blissfully alone. The one that strikes fear in your heart. Then, you don't hear it for days and just as you're lulled into a sense of complacency, it happens again.

You start to think you are hearing things. You ask your daughter, "Did you hear that weird pinging noise?!" She did, so you know you're not losing your mind . . . at least in this case. You ask her to climb around in the back of the car in the parking lot, just to make sure there isn't some strange animal in the car . . . you do live in the country after all. Nothing.

Days later you hop in your freezing-cold car and while it's still warming up and you're sitting at a light, there it is again! You turn off your heat, you turn off the car stereo, and strain to catch it . . . knowing you are going to have to drop the car off to your mechanic with a vague, "It's making a strange pinging noise but only once in a while and very randomly. Good luck!"

After a week of pinging and plinking you drive cautiously, waiting for your axle to fall off or a stray squirrel to make its way out from under the backseat. Then a snowstorm comes and you decide this snowy day would be a good time to try out that new recipe you've created, which you envision looking so sweet packed in individual jars. So you ask your daughter to grab that flat of mason jars you've had in the back of the car for a week. She treks out through the mounds of cold snow and plops the flat of jars down on the warm kitchen counter . . . and as you turn to put the cupcakes in the oven, you hear it. The distinctive *ping, ping, ping* of a dozen mason jar lids clanging against each other—the sound of you saving $1,000 in car repairs and a whole lot of embarrassment!

> If we had all the answers or lived without the many mysteries in this life, we would never draw close to or depend on Him.

Doesn't it seem like life is a little that way? You find yourself worrying about a problem that doesn't really exist. That friend who hasn't called this week; is she upset with you about something? Your teenager isn't communicating as much as usual (i.e., his "uh-huh" answers have turned to silence and you're concerned); is she in trouble at school, or is he depressed? Too often we assume the worst when the reality turns out to be far better than what we were imagining. But what about when reality isn't better than our fears?

It seems to me that the hardest situations to get through are those where there is no clear direction. We find ourselves in seasons in our lives when there seems to be a giant question mark hanging over our heads. I've often thought how much easier it would be if God would just make a big arrow appear in the sky pointing me toward the right answer. But, in His infinite wisdom, God knows that isn't what is best for us. If we had all the answers or lived without the many mysteries in this life, we would never draw close to or depend on Him.

Charles Swindoll says, "We must cease striving and trust God to provide what He thinks is best and in whatever time He chooses to make it available. But this kind of trusting doesn't come naturally. It's a spiritual crisis of the will in which we must choose to exercise faith." That seems easier said than done, right? Swindoll is acknowledging just how hard it really is when he refers to a "crisis of the will." I have found in my own life that it is usually these moments of crisis that serve to strengthen my faith in God. Those are the times when I am going to be left with two choices. I can feel frustrated about not having all of the answers exactly how and when I want them. Or I can see the crisis as an opportunity to trust God and His timing in my life. When I choose the latter, what I find time and time again is that while I might not always like the outcome, it gets easier and easier to turn to Him first when a new challenge arises.

Imagine what would happen if we stopped trying so hard to figure everything out and took our cue from the sparrow in Matthew 10:31: "So don't be afraid; you are worth more than many sparrows." The sparrow doesn't wonder where its food will come from. It knows all of  its needs will be provided for, just like God is waiting to provide for all of your needs and my needs.

After the winter there is always spring. There is always new growth and new life. There may be times when something is actually wrong, and just as we turn to our car mechanic to look under the hood and assess what repairs need to be made, we can turn to God to tell us where we need to go from here. But for those times when we are concerned about something we can't pinpoint, let's remember to cast our cares upon the One who desires to unburden us from stress and fear, and learn to rest in His provision!

THE BEAN

● ●

To the casual observer, it looked like any other ordinary houseplant. A little scraggly around the edges, sitting on my windowsill, soaking up the sunshine and warmth. One might think it was a clearance plant I had picked up from my local big-box store. You know, those plants that no one else wanted so they stopped getting watered as much, and now they are all grouped together on a cart marked 75 percent off. I always wonder if I'm the only one who feels the urge to snatch up all of those little droopy plants and bring them home, to nurture back to life.

But this particular plant wasn't a clearance plant, saved from the compost bin. This plant was extra-special. It was my girl's bean plant. Germinated from a dried-out bean, hanging out in a half-open package of beans, purchased a year ago from the grocery store. Who knows how long this little bean had been sitting around in a bag of other dried-out beans waiting to be thrown into a pot of water, cooked and eaten? That was the only hope and future that this particular bean had to look forward to.

But my daughter had bigger aspirations for that bean. She picked that one bean out of the many because she saw that it had potential. It was destined for greater things. And with tenacity, she set about revealing what really lay deep inside the core of that little legume. This is just one of the many things I love about that girl of mine. She didn't know that you can't grow a plant from a dried-out, withered-up bean meant to be cooked and eaten. She didn't know that even the freshest bean is not meant to grow in fall, outside of planting season.

She laid that little bean between wet paper towels, and tended it faithfully, giving it sunlight and keeping it damp, until one day, against all odds, a tiny sprout burst forth. While I was in complete shock at this occurrence, my daughter wasn't. She simply placed that little bean in a pot and stuck it on the windowsill in the kitchen. It was given sunlight, and water, good soil, and lots of attention. Would you believe that this little bean plant grew? And not just a little bit. It grew big! And even more amazingly, it grew new beans. It was creating new life.

> He promised that you,
> His special creation, will also
> produce fruit in your life,
> if you will just let Him grow
> you where you are right now.

Didn't this bean know it was dried out? Didn't this bean know it was October? Didn't this bean know it was in a pot and not in the ground? Didn't this bean know it was on a windowsill in a house? Didn't this bean know that one night while fumbling around in the kitchen for a glass of water someone knocked it over and damaged its stalk? Didn't this bean know it wasn't where it was supposed to be?

Didn't it know it wasn't in the perfect environment or the ideal situation? Didn't it know that the conditions weren't right for it to grow? Maybe it did. But it was going to bloom anyway. Right where it was. In spite of its circumstances. In spite of being dried out and useless. In spite of being in a temporary place and not really home. In spite of having been broken and then haphazardly tied back into place.

I think that God had a purpose for the bean. It was supposed to grow and produce new beans. Produce fruit. That was its purpose. And that is ours. To germinate what God has put in us. To thrive in all circumstances. To persevere through the dry seasons, through the times when we feel we are just one of the masses and have nothing special or unique about us.

God says in His Word, "For I know the plans I have for you, plans for welfare and not for evil, to give you a future and a hope" (Jeremiah 29:11 ESV). God has a plan for us. He created us with a purpose. If He created even a little bean to fulfill its purpose, how much more does He care about helping us fulfill ours? He calls us to have the same kind of faith my daughter had about her bean. A faith that holds fast to the belief that God will do as He promised. At the beginning of time, He created the bean and promised it would become a plant and produce fruit. And He promised that you, His special creation, would also produce fruit in your life, if you will just let Him grow you where you are right now. We need to be like the bean plant, doing what God purposed us to do. We need to forget about our surroundings. Forget about how temporary it feels. Forget about whether or not it's the right season in our life. We need to let go of the fear that we are too dried up or that we have nothing to give.

We've all heard the saying, "Bloom where you're planted." But the reality is that the little dried-out bean my daughter discovered in the pantry was never going to be able to bloom on its own. Oh sure, sometimes we may have seen an occasional sprout in that old bag of dried beans. But it was only after the bean had been planted in good soil, given plenty of sunlight and just the right amount of water, that it really began to bloom. And not just bloom, but grow and produce more beans. Like that little bean, we need to make sure that where we are planted and how we are planted gives us the best opportunity for growth. We need the healthy soil of God's love, the sunlight of the truth of His Word, and the saturation of His grace in order to not only bloom, but continue to grow into the women we were created to be.

Sometimes we need to spell it out for those we love to show them just how we feel. Mom will be grateful you did with this thoughtful gift.

ALPHABET LETTER TILES MOTHER'S DAY FRAME

SUPPLIES

_ frame
_ wooden 1-inch
  alphabet tiles
  (*found at craft stores*)
_ burlap
_ scrap fabric
_ hot glue gun

INSTRUCTIONS

1 Remove the glass from your frame and set aside. You won't be using it for this project.

2 Remove the cardboard backing. Cut a piece of burlap to fit the cardboard backing and attach it with hot glue or craft glue that won't leave a residue after drying.

3 Decide what words you want to form with your letters and arrange on the backing.

4 Use hot glue to attach them to the burlap-covered backing and allow to dry before putting it back inside the frame.

INSTRUCTIONS FOR THE FABRIC ROSETTES

1 Cut long strips of the bandanna fabric approximately 2 inches in width.

2 Tie a loose knot at the top of the strip. Tuck the ends of the fabric into the knot.

3 Pull the long end up and over the knot and then begin wrapping it around the knot, forming a petal by twisting and wrapping, twisting and wrapping, etc.

4 Tuck in the end of the fabric and secure with it hot glue.

5 For added interest, consider making these in varying sizes. To make smaller rosettes, simply use a shorter length of fabric.

THE
CHIN HAIR

● ●

When I was in middle school, a book arrived on the scene that rocked my preteen world. *Are You There, God? It's Me, Margaret* was revolutionary at the time because it addressed all of the angst that comes with being an adolescent girl. From training bras to feeling like you were the last one to get the Big P to dealing with boys who went from being just pesky to being pesky and yet strangely more appealing. Mostly I was just flabbergasted because I was one of those odd ducks who really didn't want to develop and frankly abhorred the idea of growing up in general, and the thought of purposely trying to increase your bust seemed beyond my comprehension.

Now, even though I pouted when my mom insisted I start wearing a training bra (I vividly remember sitting out on the curb in front of my house and thinking that this radical change must be so obvious that the people in every single car that drove by just *knew* that I was wearing a bra!), and even though I couldn't wait to get off that couch when "The Talk" was over, it by no means meant that

I hadn't absorbed all of this new, shocking information. But, nowhere, not in any single book or *Teen Beat* magazine or sixth grade health class, did they ever mention chin hairs. And I cry foul!

Really, someone should have warned me. Chin hairs are not "fearfully and wonderfully made." As if it isn't bad enough that I'm nearing forty and still have the occasional pimple (yet another thing that I should have been warned about), I regularly find myself horrified when the light hits my face just at the perfect angle to reveal a coarse, black nubbin of a hair (or two!) sticking straight out. I live in blissful ignorance on those dark winter days but come spring I am consistently shocked and dismayed to be sitting at a stoplight and glance in the rearview mirror only to see that I have apparently missed an entire forest's worth of chin hairs. Frankly, I've come to realize that I should have a pair of tweezers with me at all times. Like people who have to have an EpiPen with them in case of an allergic reaction.

Hear me when I say this: There is a point at which I must get up from kneeling before the throne and start walking again.

I'm quite certain that throughout the course of history as the Bible was translated, they left out one very important verse. When God is handing down the consequence of their sin to Adam and Eve and He informs them that they will now have to toil the earth for food and have pain in childbirth, the translators forgot to include, "Thou shalt also be cursed with chin hairs." The other morning as I once again reached for my trusty tweezers, I realized that one particularly annoying chin hair always grew back in the same exact spot. It was relentless. I plucked, it came back. Sometimes it would even bring a friend or two. And as I contorted my arms into all sorts of interesting positions trying to get just the right angle to pull that sucker out, I realized how much that chin hair was like sin. It can't be a coincidence that "chin" and "sin" rhyme. No matter how many times the light shines on the sin in my life and I recognize it, pluck it out, put some makeup on it, and go about my day, it seems to come back again and again. Almost always in the same place. I like to think of myself as a quick study, someone who catches on to things pretty easily. But I find that over and over again, like a stubborn chin hair, there are sin areas in my life that I think are resolved and yet they continue to resurface. Through recognition of my sin, confession, and the receiving of forgiveness I'm made new and whole. The slate has been wiped clean. "If we confess our sins, he is faithful and just and will forgive us our sins and purify us from all unrighteousness" (1 John 1:9). But even though the slate has been wiped clean, it doesn't mean that it won't get written on again. It's in our nature as humans after all. I'm so, so grateful for the grace that is extended to me over and over again. And yet, while that grace and forgiveness is given to me unconditionally, it doesn't excuse me. We often get caught up in this idea of nothing being required of us when it comes to our relationship with the Lord. But I think that can become a crutch. Hear me when I say this. There is a point at which I must get up from kneeling before the throne and start walking again. And I must walk as one who has been made new. "'He himself bore our sins' in his body on the cross, so that we might die to sins and live for righteousness; 'by his wounds you have been healed'" (1 Peter 2: 24).

One definition of *insanity* is doing the same thing over and over again, expecting different results. We sin, come before God, confess our sins, receive forgiveness, and then go on to do the exact same thing again. Insanity. Yet we know that we cannot change through our own power. So, what's the answer? Honestly, I'm not entirely sure. But what I am sure of is that in order to be truly made new, I must be willing to allow God to be the Master Plucker. You see, if I really wanted to do away with those chin hairs forever I realize that I could just do laser removal. Zap those bad boys! But my guess is that once I zapped one area, another one would pop right back up. Like in the form of long nose hairs or something equally horrible. And that's the way sin is. We might conquer one area of sin in our lives, only to realize that another has surfaced.

It would be easy here to ask, "Well, why even bother, then?" Why not just let those hairs grow willy-nilly? Well, for one thing, I'd probably end up in the circus or at the state fair, where people would win prizes trying to guess the length of my chin hair. And, for another, frankly I'm supposed to continue to grow in my faith. Hebrews 5:12 says, "In fact, though by this time you ought to be teachers, you need someone to teach you the elementary truths of God's word all over again. You need milk, not solid food!" I don't want milk anymore. I want solid food! I want God to take out those tweezers and pluck away! Will it sting? Yes. Will some of those "sin hairs" try to come back? Yes. But if I'm truly being transformed, they should pop up less and less. And even when they do, I'll know that their purpose is to serve as a reminder of my need for grace and mercy and forgiveness and . . . tweezers.

DUST

· ·

When you live in the Pacific Northwest, you develop an odd sixth sense. Perhaps it's the lack of Vitamin D, which gives us almost superhuman abilities to sense the sunshine coming our way. On one particular day in spring, I was craving warmth and light and desperately wanted the clouds to go away. It seemed that my toes and fingers were perpetually cold and my general attitude was beginning to match the seemingly permanent gray-colored sky. But on this day, I knew even before I walked into the kitchen that something had changed since the last time I had been in there. Things suddenly looked a little bit lighter and brighter. And then it happened.

Glorious rays of sunshine began streaming through the skylights, flooding the room with their glow. With a smile on my face and a spring in my step, I walked around the kitchen and just took it all in. Everything seemed to take on an almost ethereal quality. Even the sink faucets were shining brightly. But then something stopped me in my tracks. What was that in the corner? Was that a giant dust bunny I just saw? And where on earth did those spots and stains on the floor come from? I was certain I had just mopped the other day! How could I have missed them? On second thought, maybe that glorious light streaming in wasn't such a good idea. The only thing it was doing was high-lighting all the places I hadn't really cleaned. *Come back, clouds*, I thought, *come back!*

As I grabbed my broom, I couldn't help but think about how much the dust in the corners was like the dust in my heart. It had been there all along, lurking in the shadows, but I had convinced myself I had done a proper job of cleaning it up. And yet, all it took was a little bit of sunshine to reveal the truth. I guess that is the difference between picking up and deep clean-ing. Way down in the crevices of my heart are places that I have only skimmed over. Sins that have never been confessed. Fears that have never been expressed. Doubts that have never been released. I hide them away, hoping that somehow my picking up will keep me from ever having to do any deep clean-ing. I wanted to just stand and soak in the beauty of that moment

> I can confess my dirty corners to my Savior, feel forgiveness washing over me, and hopefully go forward realizing that what I really need to do is some dust management.

with the sun streaming in through my windows. Instead, I was made aware of every grimy little corner. And, as so often is the case when we come into the presence of our Savior, the difference between His shine and our grime is crystal clear.

On those cloudy days I thought I was doing a proper job of cleaning. But what I've come to realize is that there is quite a big difference between

cleaning and cleansing. Coming home from the park re-
cently, I handed an antibacterial wipe to my kids and
asked them to wash their hands off. My daughter quickly
replied, "But, Mommy, I already wiped the dirt off on
my pants so my hands are all clean now!" Her innocent
assumption that since she couldn't actually see the dirt
anymore, her hands must have been clean is one we make in our own lives.
How often do we try to simply wipe off our sin?

The word *clean* is defined as "the removal of dirt or pollution." But the
word *cleanse* is defined as "to purify." Big difference! My daughter's hands appeared to be clean because she had wiped the dirt off of them (and onto her
pants, of course!). And my house appeared to be clean because I had picked
up, lightly mopped, and skimmed the surface. But the reality was that neither her hands nor my house had been cleansed. And they certainly weren't
purified!

Second Timothy 2:20–21 says, "In a large house there are articles not
only of gold and silver, but also of wood and clay; some are for special purposes and some for common use. Those who cleanse themselves from the latter will be instruments for special purposes, made holy, useful to the Master
and prepared to do any good work." I want to be an instrument. I want to
be useful. But I can't do that unless I'm willing to allow God to do a very
thorough and very deep cleaning in my heart. And deep cleaning is a messy
process. It usually gets a lot worse before it gets better. As I clean our bath-
tubs, I notice the dirt and grime is pulled away from the sides but it doesn't
immediately go down the drain. It pools and puddles up on the bottom
and frankly horrifies me as I realize I probably should be cleaning it more
regularly. But true cleansing, true purifying, is a multi-step process.

Once I'm made aware of the sin in my life, the dust in the corners of my heart, becoming cleansed requires several steps. It's more than simply wiping off the surface. Like the moment when the sun highlighted those dirty corners in my kitchen, when I grow closer to Christ, my own dirt is highlighted. But I have to be willing to see it, to recognize it for what it is. Then and only then am I able to move on to the next steps in the purifying process. I can confess my dirty corners to my Savior, feel forgiveness washing over me, and hopefully go forward realizing that what I really need to do is some dust management. Because it's better to take the time to clean each day, even when the dust isn't as visible, than to let it reach the point where it is so piled up that it swirls around when you walk by.

When I am staying in the Word and seeking a deeper relationship with the Lord, it doesn't matter what the weather is on any given day. It won't take sunshine breaking through the clouds to highlight those dirty corners of my heart. They will be revealed along the way, and I will have the opportunity to be purified. And now, you'll have to excuse me. I spy a dust bunny and need to go get the broom.

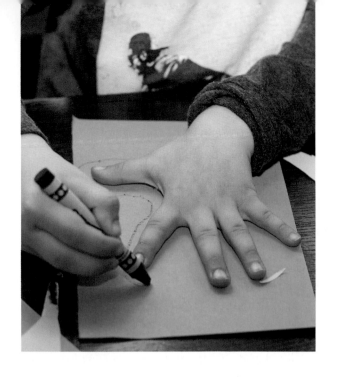

BEING
IMPORTANT

● ●

*M*oms everywhere know the truth about the gifts they receive from their children. It's not the certificate for a massage or a mani-pedi or that big bouquet of flowers that means the most. It's the stapled-together book of coupons good for a hug or maybe, if you're really lucky, cleaning up their room without complaining. Or it's the handprint framed with Popsicle sticks that immediately causes you to do the ugly cry because you know that those little hands won't stay that little forever. So when Mother's Day rolled around one year, I just knew that my mama heart was going to be filled to the brim and I was ready for them to bring on those Popsicle sticks and coupon books and even another handprint or two. My sweet girl, bless her heart, can hardly stand keeping a secret and she had been giving me little hints all week long. "Mommy, I made something for you at school today and you are going to love it!" "Mommy, I made something for you and you are going to love it and I painted it!" "Mommy, I made something for you and I can't tell you what it is but you are going to love it and I painted it and it's a bug and it's red with spots on it and it can stick to the wall!"

And while there were parts of my gift that might not have been completely surprising (like the hand-painted ladybug magnet!), there was one thing that completely caught me off guard. Instead of a card, my daughter's teacher had helped each student write out what they liked about their mom. "I wrote this about you, Mommy," she said as she handed me the card. I smiled as I saw her precious first-grade handwriting and how carefully she had written out each letter. I laughed to myself as I read the description of my hair as "brawn" and that I am "medium"-sized. My eyes welled up when I saw where she had written that I make her happy. But then, as I read the next line, my breath caught in my throat. My daughter had written, "My mom makes me feel important."

> That fixed point on the pendulum? Well, that's God. He is the equilibrium. He's the center. And our value, our worth, our importance lies in Him.

I make her feel important. It was so surprising to see that she chose that particular word. And yet, it made my heart swell with joy to think that my sweet girl knows she is important. But then . . . well, then less heart-swelling thoughts followed. *Is she getting a big head? Is she going to be one of those little girls who thinks that the world revolves around them? We don't want her thinking that she's too important, now, do we?*

You see, feeling important is something I've always struggled with. There seems to be a pendulum in our culture that swings back and forth. On the one side, you have little girls who are encouraged to believe that the world actually does revolve around them. They can do no wrong. They are

encouraged to wear shirts with the word *diva* across them in big bedazzled letters. They are so beautiful, so special, so amazing, so perfect that when anything (or anyone) challenges that image, then it couldn't possibly be through any fault of their own. Because they are so beautiful, so special, so amazing, and so perfect.

On the other side of this pendulum swing is where the "good" Christian girl tends to land. If I think I'm important, then it must mean I'm prideful and puffed up and need to pray for humility and to be taken down a notch or two or three. I need to serve more, do more, *be* more. If someone compliments me, I shouldn't just say thank you, because that would mean I really thought that I had done something that warranted praise. And that would mean I'm not humble. And then I'd need to pray for humility again—and around and around we go. You think my home is pretty? Well, let me tell you about all of its flaws and how messy it is and how that thing that looks like it cost $1,000 I actually got on clearance for a nickel but I had to turn it around so it didn't show the big scratch. In other words, let me debunk your thinking by telling you just how wrong you were to ever utter the words, "Your home is pretty." And don't even *try* to compliment me on anything having to do with my personality or my talents or my abilities or anything having to do with just *me*, because I will correct you so quickly that you will be convinced I am the biggest loser you've ever met! Can you guess on which side of the pendulum I find myself?

But here's the thing about pendulums: They are made using a fixed point. And it's this fixed point that allows them to swing back and forth from one extreme to the other while always coming back to that point. It's the equilibrium position. The center.

When our fixed point shifts, our pendulum has to work harder to get back to that fixed point. Which basically means that neither extreme is right. But, really, when exactly are extremes a good thing? I want my girl to know how amazing she is. How incredible, how special, how loved, how *important* she is. So how do I keep her from being like those kids who try out for TV talent shows when they are horrible singers but have been told all of their lives that they are the next big superstar?

And how do I keep her from being, well, like me? How do I keep her from not knowing how to take a compliment? How to not be a martyr? How to not be a people pleaser? How to fully embrace the unique talents and gifts with which God has blessed her and to use those to glorify Him with absolute confidence? Here's how: That fixed point on the pendulum? Well, that's God. He is the equilibrium. He's the center. And our value, our worth, our *importance* lies in Him.

You have searched me, Lord, and you know me. You know when I sit and when I rise; you perceive my thoughts from afar. You discern my going out and my lying down; you are familiar with all my ways. Before a word is on my tongue you, Lord, know it completely. (Psalm 139:1–4)

He knows when we sit and when we rise. He knows every thought and every word before it's even spoken. We are important to Him. We must be, right? For Him to sacrifice His one and only Son for us? (John 3:16).

I want my girl to know that as much as she is important to us (to infinity and beyond!), she is even *more* important to God. And if she is already realizing that at such a young age, then maybe we are on the right path. And maybe, just maybe, she can teach her mother a thing or two!

Welcome the month of May with these darling baskets that will give your friends and neighbors a sweet surprise when they find them hanging on their front door.

TIN CAN MAY DAY BASKET

SUPPLIES

- large metal soup or coffee can
- electric drill
- 3/16 drill bit
- spray paint (color of your choice)
- ribbon (color of your choice)
- fresh flowers
- plastic bag
- rubber band

INSTRUCTIONS

1 Clean inside of the can and remove the label on the outside, soaking in warm, sudsy water if necessary to be sure not to have anything still sticking to the surface.

2 Using your drill, make a hole on each side of the can. This is where your ribbon will be pulled through.

3 Spray the can in the paint color of your choice, making sure to work in a slow, back-and-forth motion for optimum coverage and no drips.

4 Once the can is dry, thread the ribbon through the first hole so that the end is on the inside of the can, and then tie a knot to secure it.

5 Repeat on the other side so that what you end up with is a handle for the can.

6 Place your flowers into a plastic bag and fill with enough water to cover the ends of the stems, then secure with a rubber band and tuck into the can.

7 Hang on the doorknob of a neighbor or friend's door to wish them a happy May Day. Include a little note if you would like them to know it's from you.

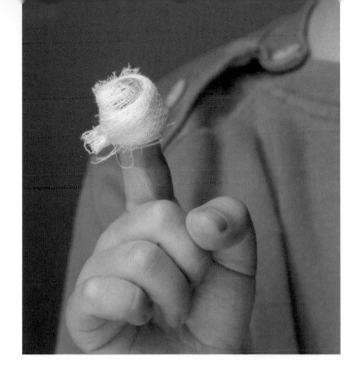

SCARS

● ●

*H*e painstakingly pointed out all his scars to me. "See this one, Mommy? I got this one when I made the contraption out of your old vacuum cleaner and cut my head on the metal tube!"

Yes, son, I remember that one vividly.

"Here's one I got when I was your age." I pointed to my bottom lip. "I fell and bit right through it!" He was fascinated and wanted all of the gory details.

"And see this one?" He excitedly pointed out another one to me, interrupting my own scar-riddled tale. "This one was from when I almost cut my finger off from slamming it in the door!"

Oh, yes. That one I remember like yesterday.

Being an eight-year-old boy, he was all about one-upping me, and being an eight-year-old boy, he had far surpassed me by now in the scar department. He took some perverse pleasure in his scars, like they were badges of honor from surviving his first years of life. To me, though, they represented fear. Fear and a melancholy, lingering sense of failure, as a parent. Failure that, in those moments, I hadn't been watching quite as closely as I should have. That I hadn't monitored these situations, and the end results had been many bandages and urgent-care visits. His scars spoke to me and reminded me of my often-lingering sense of inadequacy about my mothering.

At forty-three years old, I carry many scars. Scars you can see and many you cannot. After losing 132 pounds a year and a half ago, my body is now covered in scars—scars from stretching skin beyond its capacity. These scars on my body are an outward sign of the healing scars on my heart, and in my mind, as I acknowledge and continue to struggle with my idolatry of food. I have had feelings of deep shame when I see them. Shame at what I did to my body for so many years. Embarrassment that even though I am now at a healthy weight, I must continue to wear my past as a reminder of my sin.

> Jesus says that my scars are a reminder of overcoming, of triumphing over sin! My scars make me a conquerer and an overcomer!

Why is it that an eight-year-old boy can confidently point out and be proud of his scars, when I do my best to hide mine? To him, scars represent adventure and boldness, and a willingness to live life to the fullest, while mine represent secrecy and shame.

I have had so much praise and acknowledgment of my effort to find health in my life; on the surface, people see a woman confident in her own skin. They don't know that under the clothes my skin is damaged beyond repair, forever a reminder to me of my past.

I have found comfort in reading the words of Paul as he shares his own trial with his flesh.

So to keep me from becoming conceited because of the sur-passing greatness of the revelations, a thorn was given me in the flesh, a messenger of Satan to harass me, to keep me from becoming conceited. (2 Corinthians 12:7 ESV)

We never learn what Paul's "thorn" was, nor do I think it is relevant. What we can learn, through Paul, is that often God allows trials to be placed into our lives to remind us of our ability to conquer fleshly desires, through the grace of Christ Jesus. So that through these trials, and the reminder of them, we may remain humble and mindful of all that God has helped us to overcome—but that overcoming often leaves scars.

While Satan says that my scars are a reminder of sin and failure, Jesus says that my scars are a reminder of overcoming, of triumphing over sin! My scars make me a conquerer and overcomer!

Jesus carried His own scars as a reminder of His victory over death. He was pierced for our sins and yet rose again, His scars are a testimony to overcoming the grave for all of eternity!

In fact, He was asked to show them as proof that He was the Christ, risen.

Although Thomas the Twin was one of the twelve disciples, he wasn't with the others when Jesus appeared to them. So they told him, "We have seen the Lord!"

But Thomas said, "First, I must see the nail scars in His hands and touch them with my finger. I must put my hand where the spear went into His side. I won't believe unless I do this!"

A week later the disciples were together again. This time, Thomas was with them. Jesus came in while the doors were still locked and stood in the middle of the group. He greeted His disciples and said to Thomas, "Put your finger here and look at My hands! Put your hand into My side. Stop doubting and have faith!"

Thomas replied, "You are my Lord and my God!" (See John 20:24–28.)

The Reverend C. H. Spurgeon said so beautifully:

Nor are these only the ornaments of Christ: they are his trophies—the trophies of his love. Have you never seen a soldier with a gash across his forehead or in his cheek? Why every soldier will tell you the wound in battle is no disfigurement—it is his honor. "If" said he, "I received a wound when I was retreating, a wound in the back, that were to my disgrace. If I have received a wound in a victory, then it is an honorable thing to be wounded." Now, Jesus Christ has scars of honor in his flesh and glory in his eyes. He has other trophies He has divided the spoil with the strong: he has taken the captive away from his tyrant master; he has redeemed for himself a host that no man can number, who are all the trophies of his victories: but these scars, these are the memorials of the fight, and these the trophies, too. (C. H. Spurgeon, "The Wounds of Jesus," [sermon, New Park Street Chapel, Southwark, January 30, 1859], accessed February 3, 2016, http://www.romans45.org/spurgeon/sermons/0254.htm.)

Are we capable of seeing the scars in our lives in this way? As trophies of that fight we have won, to be displayed proudly. As memorials to what we have conquered in our own lives.

Can we identify with Jesus as He held out His scarred hands to His beloved disciples, as proof that He was *alive*? Can we see our scars as reminders of a victory over sin and not something to be ashamed of?

I pray that as you remember the wounding and death of our Savior and, three days later, His triumphant resurrection, you will also remember that He bears scars, scars that represent eternal life for you and for me! That like Jesus, when He revealed His scars to His disciples, we can reveal our scars to those around us and point to them and say, "I am an overcomer and these scars are proof of God's goodness and mercy in my life!"

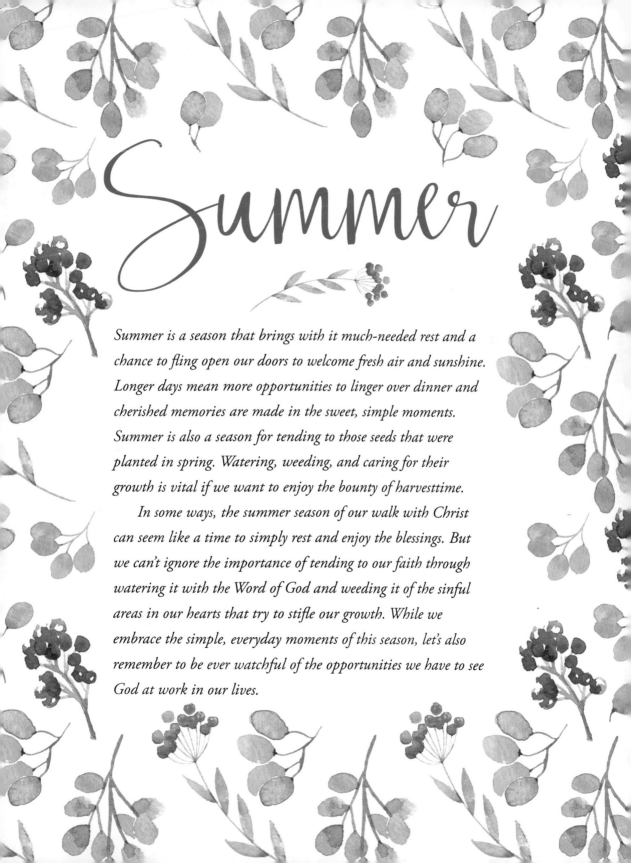

Summer

Summer is a season that brings with it much-needed rest and a chance to fling open our doors to welcome fresh air and sunshine. Longer days mean more opportunities to linger over dinner and cherished memories are made in the sweet, simple moments. Summer is also a season for tending to those seeds that were planted in spring. Watering, weeding, and caring for their growth is vital if we want to enjoy the bounty of harvesttime.

In some ways, the summer season of our walk with Christ can seem like a time to simply rest and enjoy the blessings. But we can't ignore the importance of tending to our faith through watering it with the Word of God and weeding it of the sinful areas in our hearts that try to stifle our growth. While we embrace the simple, everyday moments of this season, let's also remember to be ever watchful of the opportunities we have to see God at work in our lives.

I WILL ALWAYS COME FOR YOU

$\mathcal{I}$t was one of those summer days that was just ripe with potential. As ripe as the blackberries we passed as we walked along the path down toward the water. We crossed an old covered wood bridge and found the perfect spot to set up camp for the day. The kids eagerly approached the creek, and within minutes their flip-flops were off and they began wading in, hollering every time they spotted a crawdad. It didn't take long, though, before we realized that despite our idyllic surroundings, the current in the water was fairly brisk. I cautioned the kids to be careful and kept a watchful eye on them while chatting with my parents, who had joined us on our outing.

After basking in the warm sunshine for a while, my dad convinced my son that he should get in the water and let Papa throw the ball to him from up on the bridge. While they played, my daughter grabbed the inner tube and headed back into the water to continue her crawdad-hunting adventures. I sat back in my chair and could feel all of my muscles relax while I mentally congratulated myself on making such a perfect summer outing come to fruition. My euphoria lasted all of about one minute before I was suddenly aware that something was wrong. Very wrong.

My daughter, deciding she would rather float than wade, had tucked her feet up into the inner tube and had been happily drifting along before suddenly getting caught in the current. Within seconds she was being swept downstream. My dad, standing on the bridge, saw it happening and told my son to grab her as she floated by him. My son, unbeknownst to us, had found himself stuck in the water, tangled up in branches as he tried to find the ball they had been tossing only moments before. He reached out an arm to try and catch his sister, but just missed her. And before I knew what was happening, she was drifting out of my sight. It didn't take more than a few seconds for me to run to the edge of the creek, shed my flip-flops, and jump right into that creek with all my clothes on. My body didn't even register just how cold the water actually was, because the only thing I could think about was getting to my daughter as quickly as possible. I could hear her shouting and crying, but she was getting farther and farther away from me. And what I hadn't realized as I sat there on the bank of the creek only minutes earlier was that underneath the water were all manner of roots and branches jutting out, ready to snare anything that came their way. My legs and feet were being scraped and scratched as I clawed through the water that was only getting deeper. My clothes weighed me down and the bottom of the creek acted almost like quicksand as I tried desperately to get to my girl.

> What He promised us is that there is nowhere too far that He cannot reach us.

What felt like forever was really only a couple of minutes, and I realized that while I had jumped right into the water, my dad had begun running along the shore, through the bushes and trees, keeping his floating granddaughter in sight the entire time. And just as I was getting closer to her, the current pulled her near enough to the shore for my dad to be able to step down into the water and grab her hand. He pulled her out of the water and then pulled me out after her, and my precious girl's tears and trembling were matched by my own as we clung to each other. Soaking wet, cold, and traumatized, we trudged back toward the clearing, where we were finally able to sit down, dry off, and catch our breath.

That night, as I tucked my daughter into bed, I talked with her about what had happened. We discussed how much we were taken by surprise. How we underestimated how quickly the current was moving, and how she had done the right thing by not trying to jump out into the deep, murky water but staying in the inner tube until we could reach her. We laughed together as she remembered the sight of Mommy jumping into the water with all of her clothes on. Then she became a bit quiet before saying, "I thought you weren't going to be able to come for me. I was scared that you wouldn't get to me." And with tears in my eyes, I told her, "Sweetie, I will always come for you." She smiled and I prayed with her before kissing her good-night and leaving the room.

And as I made my way downstairs, I thought about how, in those moments of fear, we can so easily forget the promises that we've always stood upon. It boggled my mind that my daughter would ever doubt that I would do everything in my power to rescue her, to come for her. But don't I do the same thing in my relationship with the Lord? In the moment of sheer panic, when life feels completely out of control, I wonder if I will drift too far away for Him to ever be able to find me. In my humanness, I go to my default mode. I doubt, I question, I think it must be impossible for Him to be able to do what He has promised, what He has always done for me. And just like I was shocked and honestly a bit saddened that my daughter questioned whether or not I would come for her, I think that must be how God feels when we do the same to Him.

Deuteronomy 31:6 says, "Be strong and courageous. Do not be afraid or terrified because of them, for the LORD your God goes with you; he will never leave you nor forsake you." My doubting default mode is based entirely on my inability to completely trust Him and my fear of the unknown. And yet, He never promised us that our lives would be without fear or hardships. What He promised us instead is that He won't leave us or forsake us. What He promised us is that there is nowhere so far that He cannot reach us. He promised us that He would always, always come for us.

Whether you put them right into your garden or tuck them into pots, these wood-burned markers are the perfect way to give your plants that extra special touch.

BURNED WOOD ROUND GARDEN MARKERS

SUPPLIES

_ small wood slices
   (*found at craft stores*)
_ wood burning kit
_ wood dowels
   (*we used 3/16 diameter*)
_ electric drill
_ drill bit
   (*we used 3/16 size*)
_ craft glue
_ pencil

INSTRUCTIONS

1 Using the pencil, lightly write out the names of the plants you wish to label onto the wood rounds.

2 Following the directions on the package of your wood burning kit, trace your penciled words with the tool and burn them into the wood. (Applying more pressure with the tip will give you a darker look. Using a pointed nib with give you a finer line.)

3 Drill a small hole into the bottom of the wood slice. Place a dab of glue on the dowel and insert it into the hole in the wood slice. The dowel shoud fit snugly, so the top does not wobble.

4 Allow to completely dry before using.

THE WAVES
OF LIFE

Growing up in Southern California afforded me many unique opportunities as a child, especially in the seventies and eighties. It was an in-between time in America. The country stood on the precipice between peace, love, and happiness, and Reaganomics, sky-high interest rates, and power suits for women. As Californians we were definitely still basking in the glow of the hippie movement, and it overflowed even into the church scene.

During this season of our lives, our family attended church on the beach—Santa Monica Pier, Lifeguard Tower 12, to be exact. We would wear our swimsuits to church and pack a picnic lunch. After service we ate together as families and spent countless hours wading in the foam of the waves as they advanced ever closer to our "sanctuary" with the coming of high tide. It was always such a thrill to watch the local surfers ride the waves. Waiting for the swells to form, they would fearlessly paddle and instinctively, at the perfect moment, rise up on their surfboards, masters of the wave.

As children who spent every weekend at the ocean's shore, we became more and more comfortable with the sea. We would venture farther out into the waves, feeling emboldened and confident in our ability to ride the surf as it rolled its way onto the shore. I even have the honor of having been baptized in the Pacific Ocean, bodybuilder in tow to break the waves and protect me from their ceaseless pounding.

I distinctly remember the first time I felt brave enough to venture farther out from the water's edge. Out past the foam of the waves, where they break on the shore and gently glide up to the edge of the sand. It was so calm past the break. Just a gentle swell and roll, the place before the waves took form, where it was peaceful and calm. I drifted on my back, far beyond where my feet could touch, and swam through the water, confident in my ability to stay afloat. It seems like what happened next was just a split second that caught

> We forget that He is always with us, that He has never left us. That He is the Master of all that was, and is, and is to come.

me off guard, but in reality it was a pattern that was set in place since the beginning of creation. The waves began to gain strength. What had, a moment before, felt like a safe place to rest on the surface of the water, became a place of churning turmoil. I could feel the pull of the water, answering its call to nature, drawing me farther and farther out. Past where I could feel solid ground. Past where I could see the shore, past where my voice could carry to the shore with my cry for help. The undercurrent tugged at my legs as I fought the rising bitter taste of panic. Then, as the waves crashed over me, rolling me with them again and again, I found that if I stopped fighting the waves and allowed them to carry me, my feet could once again find their footing. Digging my toes deep into the sand, I pushed my head above the rolling foam and took a deep breath, the panic receding as the shoreline came into focus. What had seemed like time standing still, as I fought to stay afloat, really was just moments.

We see a similar picture painted in Luke 8.

Now on one of those days Jesus and His disciples got into a boat, and He said to them, "Let us go over to the other side of the lake." So they launched out. But as they were sailing along He fell asleep; and a fierce gale of wind descended on the lake, and they began to be swamped and to be in danger. They came to Jesus and woke Him up, saying, "Master, Master, we are perishing!" And He got up and rebuked the wind and the surging waves, and they stopped, and it became calm. And He said to them, "Where is your faith?" They were fearful and amazed, saying to one another, "Who then is this, that He commands even the winds and the water, and they obey Him?" (Luke 8:22–25 NASB)

The disciples were confident in their boat; many were fisherman who had spent a lifetime at sea, and they were in the presence of Jesus, the Creator of the very water they sailed on. What should they fear? And yet, when Jesus fell asleep, and the winds began to toss them on the waves, they immediately feared they would perish! Isn't that what we often do? We become confident in our own abilities and knowledge. We are walking confidently on the shores of our life, with our Savior. Yet, the moment we venture out into the waves of our lives, to the place where we stop hearing His voice, to those deep hidden areas where we can't feel solid ground and the waves begin to toss us about, we cry out in fear, "I am perishing,

Lord!" "Where are You, God, why have You abandoned me?" We forget that He is always with us, that He has never left us. That He is the Master of all that was, and is, and is to come.

David the psalmist said, "He set my feet on solid ground" (Psalm 40:2 NLT). Can we have faith when it seems that wave after wave is pulling us from our sure footing in Christ, that He has not left us? Do we believe He is with us, asking us to have faith that He commands the winds and churning waters of our lives to be calm? That when we have lost our footing, and the deep undercurrents of pain that we all experience are driving us further and further from the comfort of shore, He hears our cries and will return us to solid ground? Have faith that God, who spoke into being the mighty oceans that have pounded sandy shores since the beginning of creation, is the same God who created you! He is there to rebuke the waves that seek to separate you from Him and to place you on the solid ground of His grace and peace!

MOMENTUM

*J*t was the week we had waited for all summer long. The one we had saved for and planned for and made lists in preparation for—vacation week! And we were heading to one of our favorite spots in beautiful central Oregon. Once we arrived we wasted no time donning swimsuits and heading to the pool, where the kids splashed and played while my husband and I relaxed in lounge chairs like slugs. Slugs that were exhausted and happily welcomed the chance to simply sit still for a while. But even slugs have to move from time to time, so on our second day we decided it would be fun to rent some bikes and head out on the resort trails to soak up some nature.

As we neared the bike-rental facility, the kids spied all the different options available to us. Oh sure, there were just plain old bikes to rent. But this family was ready for adventure! The boys decided that they would try out three-wheelers that were basically the bike version of a go-cart, while my daughter and I selected the buggy bike. The idea was that we would sit side-by-side on a bench seat while pedaling ourselves around. With our maps in hand, we plotted our course, choosing to stay on what we thought were the more flat paths, and with great enthusiasm we headed out.

This is going to be a piece of cake, I thought. I could not have been more wrong. Somehow in all of the excitement I had not accounted for the fact that my sweet daughter's legs were not only shorter than mine, nor that she would prefer simply riding in style like a queen while her mother, the servant, did all of the pedaling. For the first little while, everything was fine. We marveled at our beautiful surroundings, spotting wildlife and laughing as we watched my husband and son race each other on their go-cart bikes. The path was nice and flat, and all I could think about was that we were making such a wonderful memory for our family.

> It's only through keeping our hope in the Lord that we are able to pedal without growing weary.

But it wasn't long before the path started to be a little less flat. In fact, it was becoming downright hilly. And soon our leisurely bike ride began to serve as a reminder of just how out of shape I was. My only consolation was that my husband and son seemed to be having a hard time too. My daughter, of course, was blissfully relaxing in the luxury of being pedaled around by her out-of-shape mother. At one point, I caught up to where my son was perched at the top of a hill. We caught our breath for a moment, and then he started down the hill with me close behind. But while he had a head start, I found that I was gaining on him quickly. You see, he was coasting down the hill while I was still pedaling. I knew what he didn't know. I knew that if I simply coasted down the hill I would never make it back up the next one. I caught up and then passed him, yelling, "Pedal, buddy, pedal! You can't just coast! You need to build momentum to get up the next hill!" But by then it was too late. He only made it halfway up the hill before he had to stop and walk his bike the rest of the way.

Momentum is an interesting thing. Part of the dictionary definition of the word says that it's "the strength or force that allows something to continue or to grow stronger or faster as time passes." In order for us to make it up those hills, we couldn't just simply coast down. We had to keep pedaling the entire time. And yet, our instinct was to rest, to take the opportunity to give our legs a break. Frankly, my legs had gone beyond simply protesting and had begun to feel like they were going to fall off. But just as I reached the point where I thought I couldn't do one more hill, the terrain leveled off. We found ourselves in a beautiful wooded area and even spied a mama deer with her baby. My legs regained feeling and we made our way back to the bike-rental facility.

Later that night we sat outside on the deck of our cabin, looking at the panoramic view of the Three Sisters Mountains and recounting all of our adventures that day. I couldn't help but think about momentum: how important it is when biking over hills and how important it is in my faith. Climbing the hills in life, the steep, challenging hills, takes so much out of me. It's arduous and exhausting, and when I've reached the top, all I want to do is coast back down. After I've been through a really difficult season in my life, the only thing I want to do is rest. I feel like I've put in my time and now I should be able to simply sit back and relax. But the truth is, when we coast in our faith, we risk having the same outcome as my son did when he coasted down that hill. In the moment, we welcome the opportunity to rest. But as soon as we start up the next hill, we pay the price. Isaiah 40:30–31 says, "Even youths grow tired and weary, and young men stumble and fall; but those who hope in the LORD will renew their strength. They will soar on wings like eagles; they will run and not grow weary, they will walk and not be faint." Losing momentum in our faith means that we won't have the strength necessary to face each new hill. And it's only through keeping our hope in the Lord that we are able to pedal without growing weary.

Sir Isaac Newton said that "an object in motion tends to stay in motion." For me, staying in motion in my faith means that there is an ongoing pursuit of knowing the heart of my heavenly Father. It's remembering that I can't rely on my own strength to get up and over those hills; I need the strength of the One who will help me feel like I'm no longer pedaling but instead, soaring on wings like an eagle.

A frugal and fun way
to decorate your table
using recycled bottles
for the patriotic summer
holidays.

RECYCLED PATRIOTIC BOTTLES

SUPPLIES

_ empty glass bottles

_ 1 can of spray paint that includes a primer

_ embellishments for the outside of the bottles (*stickers, twine, washi tape, etc.*)

_ Patriotic items to place inside of your bottles (*red, white, and blue flags and pinwheels are great options*)

INSTRUCTIONS

1 Prep the empty glass bottles by removing the labels by soaking them in warm, soapy water, then allow to them to dry completely.

2 Spray the bottles lightly with the spray paint until they are thoroughly covered.

3 Once bottles are completely dried, embellish them with stickers, twine, and washi tape in fun designs and patterns.

4 Further decorate by placing flags, pinwheels, or other festive items inside.

5 Place the bottles as a simple cluster in the center of your table, or you could elevate your centerpiece by making an easy stand using an upside-down bowl with a patriotic plate stacked on top.

THE PATH

. . . .

I made my husband promise to not go too fast. I made him promise to stay where it was safe. You see, we were riding ATVs through the desert. Normally we would be riding on one together, but this time I was on my own. I was nervous about not having him drive us, not having his strong back to hang on to. I made him promise not to go too high. I'm terrified of heights. Not just a little bit terrified, but the kind of fear where you are pretty sure there is a good chance you will pass out if you look down and see there is great potential to fall off the cliff to your death. I made him promise there would be no steep hills, no crazy detours.

He said with great conviction, "I promise I'll watch out for you." So we headed off into the desert. The desert where for miles and miles all you could see was dirt and cactus and maybe a roadrunner here and there. It seemed like the kind of place where the Mafia brings people who are never seen again. We started out slowly as I acclimated to riding by myself. My husband rode ahead and watched for cars if we reached a point where we had to cross a road. He scanned the horizon for cows and bulls, who, by the way, get their entertainment from charging four-wheelers riding through their grazing areas. He rode side by side with me, matching my slower speed, when he could have sped ahead. Eventually I could feel my muscles beginning to relax, and I realized, to my surprise, I was actually enjoying myself.

This is a piece of cake! I thought. *What was I so nervous about?* I silently questioned myself. It was sunny, the skies were beautiful, and the weather was perfect. We reached our destination, an area filled with petroglyphs. No one quite knows how old they are, just that they are very, very old. No one knows who left them or why they are there. It's been said there was a battle in the valley just below. Was this a burial spot? A ceremonial structure? Who left these drawings, and what were these people like? We discussed and pondered, sharing our ideas about what happened at that spot, so very long ago. Enjoying our stop along the path. Talking, visiting, and relishing each other's company.

> Just like I am with you. Always. Through the wide-open, easy places. Through the narrow, rough, dry, and scary places. I am always here to guide you, direct you, challenge you, and protect you.

When it was time to head back, we followed the same path back down the hill, but then he took a detour. He decided to head farther into the desert, along a wash. And a twinge of nervousness pricked at me. Suddenly we were no longer able to ride side by side. He had to go ahead to guide us along this narrow path. I sped up to keep him in my sight. I had no idea where I was. None. As my husband picked up speed, the dust began to kick up from the dry desert floor. I pulled my bandanna up over my face and chuckled to myself, knowing we looked like bandits from the Old West. Up through the wash and across the desert we trekked. He took us over several hills and around a few sharp curves, with the path getting narrower and narrower all the while.

Cactus rose up on each side, reaching out to grab our sweatshirts and jeans. I felt a moment of panic, but also exhilaration at the freedom and vastness of the terrain. There was not a soul in sight, no sign of civilization, only the two of us. I watched his back as I rode behind him. Broad, strong, capable, and confident. *How does he know where he's going?* The question kept popping up in my head. *I would be so lost. I AM so lost!* I had no clue where we were or where to go, but he kept going, riding boldly forward through that vastness. *I trust him,* I whispered to myself, more than a few times. *He knows where the path leads, and he loves me, and as long as he is with me, I am safe.*

And then another voice whispered to me, quietly, softly. *Just like I am with you. Always. Through the wide-open, easy places. Through the narrow, rough, dry, and scary places. I am always here to guide you, direct you, challenge you, and protect you.* Suddenly I was able to relax. I stopped gripping the handlebars so tightly and looked up to enjoy the wild, untamed beauty on my journey. Knowing. Knowing that my husband loved me more than life itself and would never let anything harm me. And knowing that my Shepherd and Savior loved me more than life itself and would always be there to comfort, protect, and guide me through the wide-open, smooth paths in life and through the narrow, rough, desolate paths in life.

"And I will lead the blind in a way that they do not know, in paths that they have not known I will guide them. I will turn the darkness before them into light, the rough places into level ground. These are the things I do, and I do not forsake them" (Isaiah 42:16 esv).

THE SNAIL

· ·

*I*t seems that all summer long my life revolves around one word: *watering*. For the most part, I actually really enjoy having this job. There is just something so therapeutic about watching the watering can slowly fill up. Being forced to simply stand there waiting. I haul it around to all of my potted plants and convince myself that this must count as exercise. Usually I'm all alone in these moments. Standing over the plants, offering them much-needed hydration, I relish the quiet. I do some of my best thinking and praying while I'm watering. But on one particular morning, I was in a hurry to just get it done.

It was getting to that point in the late summer when the watering starts to get tedious. Frankly I was beginning to just not really care whether things lived or died. This is a sure sign that I was ready for the next season to just get here already. I hurried out the back door, scooped up the watering can, and headed for the faucet. As I crossed the lawn, I noticed a snail working its way across the grass.

Now normally, around our house, snails and slugs are only seen as enemies that must be destroyed with copious amounts of salt lest they destroy our garden. But I was feeling benevolent (or maybe just a tad bit lazy) that morning, so I left it alone. And besides, it was heading away from the garden, not toward it. As I went about my watering routine, I kept checking back to see how the snail was progressing on its trek across our yard.

Every time I glanced over I was surprised by how much farther along it was. I mean, it was a snail. If I stood and watched it, it seemed to be moving so slowly. But if I went away and came back, the snail seemed to have covered quite an impressive distance, considering it was a snail. I wondered if it was being intentional about its goal of reaching the bark just beyond the grass. Could it see the final destination, or did it just know that it needed to keep moving forward?

> When we abide in Him, we allow our roots to grow deeper. . .
> It takes time for those roots to really be strong enough to provide security in the seasons to come.

In that moment, standing there with the watering can in my hand, I saw myself in that snail. There's a first time for everything, right? As I watched the snail inching its way along, it reminded me of where I was on my faith journey. You see, there are things in life that propel us forward very quickly. Loss, trauma, tragedy, grief. When these things occur, we are forced to jump ahead. We rapidly come to new understandings about God and His plan for our lives. I've had these kinds of occurrences in my own life. Things that have caused my faith to grow by leaps and bounds. They may have been painful, but they certainly contributed to a deeper connection with my Savior. We're told that we will experience hardship. Promised it even. "I have said these things to you, that in me you may have peace. In the world you will have tribulation. But take heart; I have overcome the world" (John 16:33 ESV).

Most of the time, though, I feel like that snail, just inching my way along on my faith journey. That particular summer found me in a season when I felt as though I had traded leaps and bounds in my faith for something slower. Something more steady. Between the peaks and valleys of life, we find ourselves on plateaus. Times when we aren't experiencing extreme highs or lows. When we are just dealing with the day-in-and-day-out stuff of life. It's in the drudgery, the laundry, the packing of lunches and shuttling kids around town, that we must be more intentional about pursuing God. During the mountaintop highs and the valley lows, we can feel as though we have no other choice but to radically cling to our Savior. And those times in our faith are so powerful, so life-changing that it's easy to think that it should always be that way. But the reality is that more of our lives are spent on the plateaus than on the mountaintops or in the valleys.

I believe that it is in the plateau times that we have to be all the more intentional about nourishing our faith. John 15:4 (ESV) says that we are to "abide" in Him. While we are in the seasons when nothing major is happening in our lives, while we are in the drudgery, we have an opportunity to build a stronger foundation in preparation for the mountains or valleys to come. When we abide in Him, we allow our roots to grow deeper. And yet it takes time for those roots to really be strong enough to provide security in the seasons to come. A solid root system doesn't just happen overnight. It can be tempting to compare the growth in the plateau seasons to the growth in the mountaintops or in the valleys, which will always make it seem like not much is happening.

But, just like that snail, I continue toward my destination, which is to be more like Christ. It seems like I'm moving so slowly, and yet if I look back, I can see just how far I've come. On this nondescript summer day I found myself rooting for a snail. As it got closer and closer to the edge of the lawn, I willed it to keep going, keep trying, keep pressing on. I so admired its dogged determination. When it finally made it to the edge of the grass and onto the bark I wanted to let out a cheer. You did it, little snail! But then, it just kept on going. Maybe the bark wasn't the final destination after all. Maybe the snail knew that the real goal wasn't so visible, so easily attained. And so, like that snail, I continue on toward my goal. There will be peaks and valleys along the way. But there will be even more plateaus. And in those times when it seems like I am only just inching along, I will remember the snail.

With the addition of this homemade natural sweetener, each sip of your iced tea will taste like the very essence of summer.

LAVENDER
SIMPLE SYRUP

INGREDIENTS

_ 1 cup of water

_ 1 cup of sugar

_ 3-4 sprigs of dried
  lavender*

INSTRUCTIONS

In a medium saucepan, combine the water and the sugar. Add the sprigs of dried lavender. Bring to a boil and then reduce heat to simmer until sugar is completely dissolved.

Allow it to cool completely.

Put a strainer over a storage container and then pour syrup mixture through in order to strain off the lavender.

Add the syrup to your favorite beverage for a lovely, natural hint of lavender with a touch of sweetness.

* This recipe can be easily adapted for other flavors like mint, rosemary, or lemon.

WEEDS & WARNINGS

*I*f you have ever watched any of the seemingly hundreds of television shows featuring people on the hunt for a new home, then you know that everyone has their own idea of what is the most important thing in a house. For some it's the perfect man cave, while others have to have a certain type of countertop. I've even seen an episode where the future home owner required a special room just for her turtle. Yes, a turtle. But when it came time for us to look for a new home a few years ago, there was one simple thing at the top of my list. Trees. Oh sure, I had in mind a certain number of bedrooms that would work for our family, and I longed for an actual laundry room, but I could have found those things in hundreds of houses around town. What I really wanted was to have a house surrounded by well-established, mature trees.

It seemed as though we had been looking at houses for years before the day when we pulled into the driveway of a home for sale in our favorite neighborhood. Rather than heading toward the front door, I made a beeline toward the side of the house, where I spotted a gate leading into the backyard. It was locked, but that didn't keep me from craning my neck and going as high up on my tiptoes as I possibly could to try to see what was just beyond the gate. And as soon as I spotted the lushness of the towering pines, the brilliant red of the maple, and the soft fluttering leaves of the cherry trees, I knew that this would be our new home. The rest of the house was secondary to the luxury of living in a neighborhood while feeling like we still had a little slice of country life.

We have gotten to know those trees very well over the years. We know that the pines not only provide us with privacy, but that they also look absolutely picturesque when covered with snow. We know that the maple really likes to show off in autumn. And we know that our cherry trees have giant blossoms in the spring that are practically the size of my head.

> Being easily frustrated, short-tempered, and angry are really only the symptoms. The disease is my distance from God.

A couple of years ago, while pulling weeds in the yard I noticed that there were some that were particularly difficult to get out of the ground. No matter how hard I pulled, I was only able to get the buds off, but it was obvious that there was no root attached to them. My determination to get rid of those weeds was only matched by the depth of the hole I began to dig. Finally, my shovel struck something hard, and I felt like I was in a pirate movie digging in the spot marked by the X on a treasure map. Only this was no treasure. I had found the roots. The enormous, sprawling roots. Our beautiful cherry tree was hiding a secret. Slowly, over time, its roots had been spreading throughout our lawn, under the deck, and along the side of the house. They had been there all along but had just now begun to sprout. These tiny baby cherry trees were just happily making their way around our yard. And all that time we had been blissfully unaware.

Those little sprouts above the surface of the dirt looked so innocent. Yet we hadn't seen them for what they really were. They were a warning of a bigger problem. A problem that was rapidly growing and spreading across our yard. Those tiny cherry tree blooms were like the symptoms of a disease. And we couldn't just treat the symptoms. We needed to recognize those warning signs for what they were and get to the root of the problem. Literally.

Sometimes in my life I'm tempted to only focus on what is visible to me on the surface of my faith. At first, it seems easier to merely treat the symptoms, the things that are right in front of me, rather than getting down to the roots. I get upset at the driver who cuts me off or frustrated that no matter how many times I remind my kids to grab their backpacks as we head out the door, I still see them entering the car sans backpacks. I shoot up quick prayers for patience and think that somehow that should cover it. But being easily frustrated, short-tempered, and angry are really only the symptoms. The disease is my distance from God. While I am only focusing on the sprouts on the surface, I'm allowing the roots of separation to grow and spread. And the roots love the darkness under the surface. They do their best work in the cool, dark places. Job 12:22 says, "He reveals the deep things of darkness and brings utter darkness into the light." The sprouts are always going to try to break through the dirt. They're stretching and reaching to get out into the light. But that usually doesn't happen until they have taken root. And our sin is no different: It is always revealed at some point.

Every article we read about how to deal with invasive roots mentioned the same thing. The only real way to deal with the problem was for the tree to be removed. It had to be taken out. Right down to the stump. And you see, it's only when we are willing to allow the Lord to dig up that sin, right down to the stump, that we will be released from the choke hold it has on us.

The cherry trees in my backyard will have to be removed soon. I'm pretty sure I'll cry that day. But I have a sneaking suspicion that the grass under them, which has always struggled to grow, will begin to flourish. And the lush green lawn will remind me of what can happen when we are willing to get to the root of the problem.

STAY IN YOUR LANE

· ·

J think it is fairly safe to say that, had I known exactly what would be involved with having our son participating in the summer swim team, I might have encouraged him to take up a different sport. I'm pretty sure that even underwater basket weaving would have been preferable. That first season I felt myself in awe of and readily willing to bow down to all of the swimming families who I knew had been at it for many years. Every Saturday morning would find us up at the crack of dawn, bleary-eyed, clutching our coffee cups. We huddled together, ready to cheer on our kids for the entire minute or so that they were actually participating, while the rest of the time we ate snacks and sat around waiting for the next event. We would stand up and yell out our encouraging words like maniacs, all the while knowing full well that there was no way our kids could actually hear us when they were in the water. So basically we were just a bunch of parents cheering for the sake of each other in order to prove that despite our grumpy, early morning attitudes, we did, in fact, support and love our children.

By our second year we felt like we had graduated from our amateur status and saved our cheering for primarily those moments when the kids were standing on the starting block or just getting ready to touch the wall at the end of the event. As we became a bit quieter, we found ourselves experiencing a whole new side of the sport. You see, unlike other sports, when it comes to the mayhem of swim meets, you often feel like you are missing out on many of the nuances. There are so many kids and so many events and so many people coming and going that you feel fortunate if you actually manage to cheer for the right kid at the right time. Quieting down a bit not only saved our voices, it also allowed us to be more in tune with our surroundings.

> It's been said that comparison is the thief of joy. It robs us of the confidence we have in the truth that we were uniquely created by a loving God and put in our lane for a purpose.

One particularly hot Saturday morning it was all we could do to not jump in the water and swim alongside our kids in an effort to cool off. I found myself dreaming of drinking iced tea under a palm tree on a beach somewhere, but was quickly brought out of my reverie by shouting from my son's coach. He stood at the end of the lanes cheering on the girls from our team competing in that event when suddenly I heard these words being yelled out: "Don't look at the other lanes! It's slowing you down! Focus on your lane!" I looked up in time to see one swimmer backstroking her way to the finish line but peeking every now and then to size up her competition. Every time those pink goggle–clad eyes glanced over at the swimmers in the lane next to her, she lost a little bit more ground. And sure enough, her fingers touched the wall just slightly behind the others.

It's so hard to resist, isn't it? That temptation to com-
pare ourselves to those around us is always there. From
the moment we are born, our vital statistics are put into
a system by which we are then charted and compared to
our peers. I'll never forget bringing my newborn son to the
pediatrician for the first time. I watched as he was weighed
and measured and the numbers plugged into the computer. The doctor came
into the room and showed me exactly how he stacked up against other newborn baby boys. Suddenly my precious, unique child, who I was so certain
was the most incredible baby ever born, was reduced to a dot on a chart. Did
he fall above the line, below the line, or exactly on the line? How did he rank?
Which category did he fit into?

From scripture we know that this tendency to compare ourselves to each
other has been a struggle throughout all of history. "But when they measure
themselves by one another and compare themselves with one another, they
are without understanding" (2 Corinthians 10:12 ESV). You see, when we
compare ourselves to those around us, we allow them to define our worth.
They become our barometer, our standard. And the things we see as our
shortcomings are measured against their strengths. Every day we are slammed
with opportunities to compare. There's the mom in the carpool line who
somehow manages to look chic in workout clothes while you, on the other
hand, find yourself wearing whatever landed on the floor the previous night
as you crawled into bed. There are those Facebook status updates showing
the happy couple out on the town trying the latest restaurants while you are
standing at the kitchen sink eating what's left of the chicken nuggets on your
child's dinner plate.

Just like the swimmer on that hot Saturday morning, looking over to see
how others are doing in their lanes only serves to slow us down in our own

lane. It's been said that comparison is the thief of joy. But I think it steals so much more than just our joy. I believe it robs us of the confidence we have in the truth that we were uniquely created by a loving God and put in our lane for a purpose. "I praise you, for I am fearfully and wonderfully made. Wonderful are your works; my soul knows it very well" (Psalm 139:14 ESV). Playing the comparing game causes us to miss out on the opportunity to praise God for how He has created us. It's virtually impossible to focus on our own finish line when we are constantly peeking over to check on the progress of those around us. But when our soul knows—really, really knows—just how wonderfully made we are, suddenly those other lanes begin to fade. And we can glide through the waters of life secure in the love of our heavenly Father.

Capture a memory from the beach with a framed monogram letter made with seashells collected from the sandy shoreline.

FRAMED SEASHELL MONOGRAM

SUPPLIES

_ small seashells
_ unfinished wood frame
_ paint
  (color of your choice)
_ paint brush
_ burlap
_ twine or ribbon
  (color of your choice)
_ hot glue gun

INSTRUCTIONS

1 If your frame is unfinished, paint it in the color of your choice and allow to dry completely.

2 Cut a piece of burlap to fit the inside of the frame and secure in place with hot glue. Don't worry about the edges being perfect because you will be covering them up in the next step.

3 Use twine or ribbon in the color of your choice and attach with hot glue to the edge of the frame being sure to overlap the burlap and cover the raw edges.

4 Decide on your letter and select your seashells. Arrange seashells in the shape of your letter and then secure in place with hot glue.

5 For a fun finishing touch, hot glue another seashell to the corner of the frame.

RITUALS & RELATIONSHIPS

When I was a little girl, my bedtime routine bordered on being almost ritualistic. Okay, it was totally ritualistic. I craved continuity. Perhaps moving to different states several times added to this need, but after experiencing my own children's desire for bedtime traditions, I have to think that it is actually something ingrained in all kids. The closet doors had to be completely shut, while the bedroom door had to be left open. My stuffed animals had to be lined up along the wall by my bed in a very specific order, as they took turns being the chosen one to sleep next to me. I wouldn't have dreamed of leaving any of them out, so this was my best solution for keeping things fair and equitable among my stuffed friends.

Once the pajamas were on, the teeth were brushed, and the bedtime story was read, my dad would say good-night to me before my mom finished things off with a song. The same song. Every night. Then, after she had prayed with me and kissed me on the forehead, she would leave the room, being sure to keep the door open at exactly the place where I felt the proper amount of light from the hallway could be viewed from my bed. These rituals were supposed to give me comfort. They were supposed to provide me with a sense of security. And yet most nights, while my parents were exiting the room, something else was entering.

I would lie there on my pillow with my chosen stuffed animal tucked into the crook of my arm and the light streaming into my room, and what should have been the time when I would slip into a peaceful slumber was actually the moment when the anxiety would hit. Irrational fears would flood my mind, and my heart would pound so hard and so loudly that I was certain my parents would be able to hear it in the next room. The rituals that were supposed to calm me down and help me prepare for much-needed rest were quickly replaced with ones involving my deepest worries. Was there someone hiding in my closet? Under my bed? Would my parents be killed in a car accident? Would I wake up in the morning and the rapture would have occurred, leaving me behind because somehow I messed up when I asked Jesus into my heart?

> When ritual replaces relationship, we have a problem. So often we can find ourselves simply going through the motions in our faith.

These thoughts would race through my mind and I would desperately try to count sheep or sing a song or tell myself a story, all to no avail. But there was one thing, one amazingly simple yet incredibly powerful thing that would help to calm my mind and slow my heart rate. I would lie as quietly as possible and strain my ears, hoping, willing to hear the one sound that would bring me some comfort. The sound of my parents. Whether my mom was cleaning up the kitchen or my dad was making a phone call. It didn't really matter whether I could actually hear what they were saying. Just the sound of them moving around the house, the low mumble of their voices, gave me such a deep sense of security. My body would start to relax, my mind would stop racing, my heart rate would slow, and I would slip into a deep sleep, knowing that I was safe.

Many times throughout my journey as a Christ-follower, I have found that I've looked to the rituals of my faith to provide me with that same sense of security I longed for as a child at bedtime. Stuffed animals, night-lights, and bedtime stories were replaced with praying before meals, doing devotions, and never missing a Sunday church service unless I was deathly ill. These rituals were what I would cling to when life felt particularly unsteady. On the days when I basically felt nothing, these established routines often offered me much-needed stability. But when ritual replaces relationship we have a problem. So often we can find ourselves simply going through the motions in our faith. We live in such a culture of busyness that there isn't much room in our day-to-day lives to hear God's voice. Praying before meals, five-minute devotions, and church on Sunday mornings are not bad things in and of themselves. But on their own, these things will never lead us to a deeper personal relationship with Christ.

In Mark 7:6–8 (NASB) the Pharisees ask Jesus why His disciples didn't wash their hands according to the Pharisee tradition. Jesus replied to them, "Rightly did Isaiah prophesy of you hypocrites, as it is written: 'This people honors Me with their lips, but their heart is far away from Me. But in vain do they worship Me, teaching as doctrines the precepts of men.' Neglecting the commandment of God, you hold to the tradition of men." The Pharisees fell into the trap of placing a higher

value on ritual than they did on relationship. They forgot what it was like to have their hearts close to God.

As a young girl trying to fall asleep, it wasn't the night-light or the bedtime songs or the storytelling that would actually calm my racing mind and soothe my frightened heart. Only the sound of my parents talking would lull me to sleep. It was in hearing their voices that I found the deep sense of security I longed for. And in my journey as a Christ-follower, I have found that no ritual or tradition has ever been able to come close to the comforting sound of the voice of my Savior. Do the rituals sometimes provide an avenue by which to hear His voice? Absolutely! But nothing can compare to the feeling of being in His presence. Only in His presence can my spirit be truly at peace. And it's there that I am able to find the rest my soul longs for. Rest that is as sweet as the rest I felt as a little girl falling asleep to the sound of my parents' voices.

BERRY PICKING

As she leaned in, on her tiptoes, to get to the very best that were slightly out of reach, her footing slipped. She grabbed a branch for support, but it snapped back and she watched, in one of those slow-motion scenes that you are aware of but yet are powerless to do anything about, as the branch hit her bucket and she saw her hour of labor tumble into the mud below.

Our mom grew up on a farm. For a farm girl, growing and harvesting food was a part of everyday life. One of her favorite activities as a child was the task of berry picking. Especially blackberries. Of course, the dense branches and thorns weren't fun to navigate, but anticipating the blackberry jam and the homemade blackberry pie that her mother would make from the fruits of her labor was worth the scratches obtained from going deep into the blackberry bushes to get the largest and juiciest berries. She would carry those treasured tin buckets up the hill to the farmhouse to ceremoniously deliver them, the taste of fresh blackberry pie already on her lips.

Finding herself, many years later, retired and living on the coast of Oregon, far from that Michigan farmhouse, she felt the surreality of it all as she carried her bucket down the road to the large hedge of blackberry bushes she had spotted at the foot of their drive. She longed for the familiarity of the past. Past homes, past relationships. There's comfort in the known, and this latest adventure felt so unknown. Our mom and nostalgia are interchangeable. From the time we were little girls she taught us to love the familiar. Memories of past events and holidays were imprinted upon our hearts to be cherished and valued.

> God is all about the new! This could not be more clearly manifested than in the gift of his Son! "Therefore, if anyone is in Christ, he is a new creation. The old has passed away; behold, the new has come."
>
> 2 Corinthians 5:17 ESV

Blackberry picking felt like a nod to all she had left behind and the familiarity of it brought comfort to her. The first blackberry bush she came to ran alongside a large ditch on the dirt road. Filled with mud and debris as only a good rain-soaked Oregon ditch can be, it presented an obstacle to her berry-picking endeavors. Leaning over the ditch and stretching as far as she could, she started gathering those cherished little jewels. Collecting them gave a feeling of comfort as she remembered those childhood days, when one berry made it into her mouth for every one that made it into the bucket. Then she stumbled, and watched with dismay as the branch that should have given support knocked her entire bucket into the mud below.

Quickly bending to pick the berries out of the ditch, her frustration grew as her efforts to salvage her harvest produced more mud, leaves, and twigs in the bucket than it did fruit.

Do you often feel like this? That in your effort to salvage the past you can end up bringing dirt and debris into your life. As humans, we long for the familiar. Nostalgia is a very real feeling and while there is nothing innately wrong with remembering and reflecting on past homes, events, and friendships, trying to dust off the past and carry it into your future, often brings along discontent and disillusion for where you are in the present. When we live too much in our past life, we cannot make room for what God wants to do with us in this present life.

This is where the Israelites found themselves. After being saved by their God, we see them grumbling about their circumstances again and again. Even lamenting to Moses that they would have been better off in Egyptian enslavement.

The Israelites are reminded of what God did for them, when He birthed their nation, and what He will do for them as they prayed for deliverance from Babylon. "Remember not the former things, nor consider the things of old. Behold, I am doing a new thing; now it springs forth, do you not perceive it?" (Isaiah 43:18–19 ESV).

The Jews are being told that they should not live in the past but should look for God to bring them a new exodus.

As Mom knelt there by the side of the road, attempting to brush off her beautiful berries, she found that the harder she worked to remove the dirt, the more it seemed to work its way into the cracks and crevices. They were never going to be truly clean. Do you often find yourself spending a lot of emotional and mental energy trying to "clean up" the past? Trying to make sense of it? Mulling it over and over in your mind until the memories are so tainted that they no longer represent the truth?

You are a new creature! Don't let past hurts and pain cause you to miss out on all the new joys that God has for you!

He wants to do a new work in us, and through us, and that can only be achieved when we are living in the here and now. God is placing people in your path right now. Who are you not seeing because you are keeping your eyes on the past and not in the present? Who are you shutting out presently in your life, because you were wounded in the past, and you are allowing the mud and grime from that past relationship to cling to new ones?

Equally important, we must be careful not to allow past victories in Christ to sustain us. This can create a sense of pride that works its way into our lives. Too often we, as Christians, use our past accomplishments as an excuse to not continue on the mission to further the gospel. We rest on our ministry laurels and lose sight of all that is still before us.

Paul paints a beautiful picture of this in Philippians: "Brothers [sisters], I do not consider that I have made it my own. But one thing I do: forgetting what lies behind and straining forward to what lies ahead, I press on toward the goal for the prize of the upward call of God in Christ Jesus" (Philippians 3:13–14 ESV).

Paul is telling us that we must continue to progress in our Christian living, continually reaching ahead to see God's kingdom expanded. How can we do this when we are constantly looking behind us?

When Mom realized that there was no way to make these particular berries clean again, she turned away from them and continued down the path. As she turned the corner, there before her was another blackberry bush, this one with branches loaded and spilling over with ripe, beautiful berries right at eye level. With ease this time, she filled her bucket to the brim. God wants to do this for you, and for me, if we are willing to leave the past behind and strive toward the new!

With a simple made-from-scratch piecrust and fresh blackberries, our grandmother's old fashioned blackberry pie is the perfect summer treat.

BLACKBERRY PIE

INGREDIENTS
PIECRUST

_ ½ cup canola oil

_ 2 Tbs. milk

_ 1 Tbs. sugar

_ ½ tsp. salt

_ 1½ cups flour

FILLING

_ 3-4 cups of fresh blackberries*

_ 1 cup sugar

_ 2 cups water

_ Dash of salt

_ 3 Tbs. cornstarch

_ 3-oz. package of blackberryJell-O*

INSTRUCTIONS
PIECRUST

Mix together oil, milk, sugar, and salt. Add 1½ cups flour. Stir until it crumbles.

Press with fingertips into bottom and sides of 8" or 9" pie pan. Do not prick bottom.

Bake 10–12 minutes at 375° F until very light brown. Cool.

FILLING

Combine sugar, water, salt, and cornstarch.

Cook over low heat, continuously whisking until thick. Remove at once.

Mix in 3-oz. package of blackberry Jell-O. Mixture must be cooled but not firm.

Put a small amount of mixture in cooled crust. Layer fruit and mixture and allow to set in refrigerator until firm. Top with whipped cream (if desired) before serving.

* This recipe can be easily adapted with strawberries and strawberry Jell-O.

ONWARD, CHRISTIAN SOLDIER

We marched in sync, our little legs pumping up and down in time to the beat. We swung our arms back and forth with each step we took. "I may never fight in the infantry, ride in the cavalry, shoot the artillery! I many never fly o'er the enemy, but I'm in the Lord's army!"

We were brave soldiers standing in front of our child-size folding chairs, marching off to war, in defense of our faith! It was so easy to feel bold and confident standing there in that little Sunday school room.

I have often thought about how a soldier must feel when fighting the battle actually becomes a reality. Does he feel as David did when he cried out to the Lord, "Deliver me from my enemies, O my God; Set me securely on high away from those who rise up against me" (Psalm 59:1 NASB).

While his human nature compels him to run from danger, he is a soldier and he is committed to the mission. By enlisting in the service of his country, he has made known his willingness to die in defense of the freedom of others.

There is a chance of being wounded, of the spilling of life-giving blood . . . and yet he remains steadfast and faithful on the battle line. He does what is expected of a good soldier. While the blood of the patriot is precious, how much more life-giving was the blood spilled on our behalf, two thousand years ago, when the most precious blood that has ever flowed through human flesh was poured out to give humanity freedom from the bondage of sin?

Do you see Jesus as a warrior Savior? Sent to defend us from the enemy and to sacrificially and willingly die for us? Do you see yourself as a soldier for Christ? Because that is how Christ sees you!

Are you prepared to be both a good and faithful soldier, like Paul admonished Timothy to be? "Join with me in suffering, like a good soldier of Christ Jesus. No one serving as a soldier gets entangled in civilian affairs, but rather tries to please his commanding officer" (2 Timothy 2:3–4).

Paul is asking Timothy to soldier with him in the battle for men's souls! Could there be a more worthwhile cause for the believer?

A good soldier must be a great follower.

> Here's the good news:
> Even when we feel defeated and beaten down, even if we feel more conquered than conqueror, even when our armor feels battered . . .
> we are still the victors!

He is willing to take commands and instruction from his commanding officer, putting faith in the knowledge that his commander has been placed in leadership for a reason. The good soldier must see his role in the bigger picture and sacrifice selfish gain in defense of the greater good.

Is this something you are willing to do? Do you submit to the leadership of those in spiritual authority over you? Even more important, have you submitted your fleshly, sinful heart to the authority of Jesus Christ?

We can identify with Christ, as the ultimate Victor and Conqueror over sin, when we see ourselves as soldiers in the faith and, like every well-prepared soldier, we are provided with the armor we need. We must remember that we do not war against men, but "against principalities, against powers, against the rulers of the darkness of this world, against spiritual wickedness in high places" (Ephesians 6:12 KJV).

Our enemy is not our fellow man, but the current ruler of this earth. To defeat him we must put on the armor that we have been provided in Christ Jesus. God has provided us with the defense that we need. "Put on the full armor of God, so that you can take your stand against the devil's schemes" (Ephesians 6:11).

Here's the good news: Even when we feel defeated and beaten down, even if we feel more conquered than conqueror, even when our armor feels battered . . . we are still the victors! Because Jesus has already fought the battle and won!

In Revelation we see the triumphant return of the warrior Savior of the world and His army, which is you and me!

I saw heaven standing open and there before me was a white horse, whose rider is called Faithful and True. With justice he judges and wages war. His eyes are like blazing fire, and on his head are many crowns. He has a name written on him that no one knows but he himself. He is dressed in a robe dipped in blood, and his name is the Word of God. The armies

*of heaven were following him, riding on white horses and dressed in fine
linen, white and clean. (Revelation 19:11–14)*

As a soldier for Christ, that is worth rejoicing over!

A good soldier must also be a great leader.

A great leader does not use his position of authority to abuse those under
him. We must be oh, so very careful to lead from a place of humility and
grace, when we serve in a leadership role in the Lord's army. There isn't room
for pride in the ranks of soldiers for Christ. We must not forget, as leaders,
who is ultimately in command. We must never refrain from submitting to
the authority and teachings of Jesus Christ, in pursuit of our own fleshly
desires to be seen as a Christian leader.

Like a mighty army moves the church of God;
brothers, we are treading where the saints have trod.
We are not divided, all one body we,
one in hope and doctrine, one in charity.
(Onward, Christian Soldiers)

Nothing will divide a regiment of soldiers faster than confusion of the
mission, and nothing will divide the Lord's army faster than disunity and
strife among brothers and sisters in Christ. We must remain as, "one body,
one hope, one doctrine and one charity" as Christian soldiers!

The greatest leader in Christ's army will be found most often on their
knees in prayer and supplication for the strength to persevere and fight the
good fight! As the soldier takes time to prepare his equipment for battle, we
must also prepare ourselves for spiritual battle by being in the Word.

Let us do honor to the sacred blood poured out onto the battlefield by our Savior, by being like Paul and Timothy: good soldiers striving daily to please our commanding officer, Jesus Christ.

Autumn

The carefree days of summer are slowly beginning to blend into the winds and whispers of falling leaves. Fall is a season when days are getting shorter, and we look forward to gathering together in our homes to celebrate the harvest. The changing of leaves and their subsequent fall to the ground is a reminder that life, too, brings many changes and that, no matter how much we would like to, we can't slow down the passing of time.

As Christ-followers, we must take our cues from the falling leaves and remember that it is only through dying to our old ways that we are able to fully reap the blessings of the harvest God has waiting for us. And as we gather together to celebrate with thanksgiving all that God has provided, we are ever mindful of our deep and abiding need for His mercy and grace.

THE STANDINGS

⬤ ⬤

*F*all represents so many things. It signals the trees to shed their leaves and people to dig out sweaters tucked into the backs of closets. It means backpacks and school buses. It's the season of pumpkin everything, from lattes to candles and, of course, pie! In our family, it is the beginning of something else as well: college football. Most importantly, University of Alabama football.

See, we're a little crazy around here for Alabama football—actually, make that *a lot* crazy. In fact, there's a saying, "You don't know how crazy Southern women are until college football starts." To this I take no offense, for if you could see my mother-in-law and me on game day, you would know that truer words have never been spoken. We've been known to scream ourselves hoarse at the TV, as if through sheer volume we could make the referees hear our opinions on their play calling. We've even been known to jump up and down on furniture, which for any other occasion except for a football game, in a Southern home would be highly frowned upon.

For months we talk three-point conversions and roughing the passer. Words like *Heisman, huddle,* and *halfback* can be heard in everyday conversation around our home and every Saturday morning is spent with a cup of coffee and *College GameDay.*

Yes. Game day is a big deal around here. We treat it with a level of celebration normally reserved for birthdays, snow days, and the last day of school. It's the day every college team, across the country, enters the arena but only half will emerge victorious.

Yet, there's a day of the week that, for the serious college football fan, is equally important. That's Tuesday, the day teams are ranked on their performance that week. Each week teams move up and down. A team that was number one for months might find itself at number twenty-five, after just one loss. Everything is at stake for these teams based on their standings, determined by a board whose sole purpose is to decide who is "the best."

> Our standing . . . our value . . . our worth has already been decided. It was decided on a tree on a hill, by a man who was God.

Do you ever feel like that in your Christian walk? You have those seasons when you feel on top of your faith game! You're attending church every time the doors are open. You are reading your Bible daily and involved in three different life groups. You witnessed to your neighbor, coworker, and the grocery store cashier . . . all in one week. You're feeling number one in the Christian rankings! Then there are those seasons when your faith doesn't even feel the size of a mustard seed. Maybe you had your feelings hurt by someone at church and you find yourself making excuses not to attend, in an effort to avoid facing the pain of confronting them. Life becomes overwhelming and your schedule is full, so Bible study attendance drops off. Fear of rejection keeps your mouth closed when you are presented with opportunities to share the love of Jesus, and shame creeps in as a result.

You feel the grip on your number-one standing slip as you mentally move yourself further and further down the rankings.

The psalmist David felt the crippling effect of defeat and cried out to God. "I am bowed down and brought very low; all day long I go about mourning. . . . I am feeble and utterly crushed; I groan in anguish of heart. . . . My heart pounds, my strength fails me; even the light has gone from my eyes" (Psalm 38:6, 8, 10).

King David should have been feeling like he was ranked number one in God's eyes. He was the king of Israel and God had even called David a man after His own heart! Yet, these words in Psalms show that David wasn't feeling like number one. In fact, David wondered if God even saw him anymore. "My God, my God, why have you forsaken me? Why are you so far from saving me, so far from my cries of anguish?" (Psalm 22:1).

Are you feeling like David? Crying out to God, feeling forsaken and alone. Struggling to find your place, your footing, your standing in the world. A world that judges you on your performance, instead of your intentions. Do you feel at the top of your game one week, carrying the ball to the end zone, and then the next week tackled by life, lying under the crushing pile of worries and doubt? Maybe you've had the wind knocked out of you one time too many, and you decide it's not worth it to even play the game anymore.

Let me share something with you, my friend. Our standing . . . our value . . . our worth has already been decided. It was decided many, many years ago. It was decided on a tree on a hill, by a man who was God. He took on our enemy, in the greatest arena that has ever existed . . . and he *won*!

"There is therefore now no condemnation for those who are in Christ Jesus" (Romans 8:1 ESV).

He did this so your judgment would be covered by His sacrifice. He did this so your mistakes and failures would no longer determine your standing in the kingdom of God.

"[All] are justified and made upright and in right standing with God, freely and gratuitously by His grace (His unmerited favor and mercy), through the redemption which is [provided] in Christ Jesus" (Romans 3:24 AMPC).

There is just one rank, and one rank only, that has been given to you, my sister in Christ, and it is as the daughter of the one true King. Stand fast in that knowledge and know that this week, and the next, and the next, your worth has already been established, once and for all.

A handmade tray created
from wooden rulers is the
perfect "back-to-school" gift
for that favorite teacher in
your child's life!

BACK-TO-SCHOOL RULER TRAY

SUPPLIES

- 13" X 10" unfinished handled craft tray *(found at craft stores)*
- 12 12" wooden rulers
- Wood stain
- Craft paint *(color of your choice)*
- Wood glue
- Satin finish varnish *(optional)*
- Small handsaw
- Pliers

DIRECTIONS

1 Paint entire tray with 2 coats of craft paint in the color of your choice and allow to dry completely.

2 Carefully remove metal edge of each ruler using pliers.

3 Measure each ruler to fit snugly inside bottom of tray, and using small handsaw, cut to size.

4 Stain each ruler with wood stain color of choice and allow to dry.

5 Using wood glue, place rulers side by side in the bottom of the tray. (twelve rulers should fit perfectly within a 13" X 10" tray.)

6 For durability you can spray entire tray with a coat of satin finish varnish.

THE VINE

· ·

I hate to admit it, but I'm pretty sure that I take for granted just what a privilege it is to live in such a beautiful part of the country. I get to claim the Willamette Valley in Oregon, with its rolling hills, farmland, vineyards, orchards, and incredible mountain ranges in the distance, as my home. Yes, we have cities. But somehow they seem to take a backseat to the rest of the landscape, and frankly, I think we get spoiled. A few years ago, I flew to Arizona to visit my parents and on the return flight home I was once again struck by just how lush and green this incredible state is. Perhaps it was the days spent in the hot, dry desert that made it feel as though I was being doused with cool, refreshing water simply by staring out of the airplane window.

One of my great delights in life is that the route I take to deliver my children to their respective schools winds through all of those rolling hills, farmland, vineyards, and orchards. And throughout the course of the school year, it's as though we are getting daily visual reminders of just what happens when one season unfolds into another. In those early days of school, we are still seeing signs

121

of summer. Crops are reaching the height of their growth, basking in the warmth of the late-summer heat. The leaves on the trees have gotten as green as they're going to get, and you can actually see the grapes dangling from the vines in the vineyards. But in a matter of weeks, the signs of fall are working their way through the landscape.

On a cool morning in early October, we were headed down the winding road toward my son's middle school. It sits on forty-five acres in the middle of farmland, and although I'm nursing my coffee on the way, the time we spend driving there has become sacred to me as it gives me much-needed precious time with this growing young man of mine. This particular morning we were noticing how everything seemed aglow with red and gold, and we kept count of the number of trucks that passed us laden with pumpkins on their way to be gutted and stuffed into cans.

> Just as grapevines are trained to grow around the wires, as we grow in our faith in Christ, our hearts are being trained to reflect His.

He was gazing out the window as we passed the first of several vineyards and as he leaned forward to get a closer look he said, "Hey, Mom, do the vines grow in that shape all on their own?" I glanced over to take a look and replied, "No, buddy. You see, under those vines are wires that have been shaped into that form and the vines are growing around the wires. The wires train them in the way they should grow." And in my groggy, not properly caffeinated state of mind, I didn't really think anything more about the conversation until I had dropped him off at school and was heading back toward home and once again passed the vineyard.

As I caught another glimpse of the vines, I couldn't help thinking about the care that was involved in getting them to grow just right. They didn't just come to be like that all on their own. There was planning involved. There was intention and purpose. Someone formed those wires into the shape that has been proven for centuries to create optimum growth potential. And then, as the vines began to spring from the earth, they were carefully trimmed and trained to wind their way around those wires.

Ephesians 5:1–2 says, "Therefore be imitators of God, as beloved children. And walk in love, as Christ loved us and gave himself up for us, a fragrant offering and sacrifice to God" (ESV). Our efforts to become more like Christ can often seem impossible. We start out in our faith as these small seedlings. Planted with so much hope and expectancy and yet, like those first baby grapes, any fruit we may produce seems to be more tart than sweet. It needs time to ripen, to mature. Grapevines need to be attached, secured to something strong in order to properly grow. Those grapes dangling down are heavy in all of their lush ripeness. They need support or they will bend and break under their own weight. Just as grapevines are trained to grow around the wires, as we grow in our faith in Christ, our hearts are being trained to reflect His. The wires underneath the vines twist and turn. They go up and down. And the vines reach and stretch to follow along, becoming one with the wire. These observations have made me more curious about grapevines and in my research I discovered that one of the most important reasons for the wires is so that the vines will grow upward, away from the ground and the risk of disease. Their connection to the wires provides them with protection from what could potentially destroy them.

At bedtime not too long ago, my son and I were having a conversation about why we continue to imitate Christ even when we know we will never be able to measure up to His perfection. Frankly, it's something I've thought of many times throughout my own faith journey and I was very honest with him, as I always am, about not having all of the answers. But when I think about his question and I think about those grapevines, the only thing that makes sense to me is that while the grapevines won't ever actually become the preformed wires, they continue to take on their shape. So, while I know that in my fully human state, I will never reach the point of becoming completely Christlike, I continue to reach and stretch to take on His shape, to form my life to His. And I trust that with the proper pruning and trimming and by continuing to grow upward away from the disease of sin, my life will bear gloriously ripe fruit. Fruit that is just as full of flavor as the grapes dangling from the vines that we pass by each day on our way to school.

ENOUGH

● ●

*T*he alarm blares and my eyes struggle to open. Immediately my mind is flooded with thoughts about the day ahead. Will there be *enough* time to get it all done? I shuffle my feet along the carpet, willing my body to go toward the bathroom door rather than turning back toward the warmth of my bed. The darkness outside only contributes to my sense of grogginess. It's morning, but daylight saving time has yet to end so it feels more like the middle of the night even though it's 6:00 a.m. Coming down the stairs and into the kitchen, the first things to greet me are the dishes in the sink from last night's dinner.

There wasn't *enough* time or *enough* energy to wash them before going to bed.

We race through our morning routine of drinking coffee, packing lunches, drinking more coffee, getting homework into backpacks, drinking even more coffee, and getting out the door with coffee cup in hand. I drop my kids off at school, and as I get back in the car I can't help but wonder if I am doing enough for them. Are they getting *enough* of what they need? Am I equipped *enough* to be the mom they need me to be? Back home again, where the row of laundry baskets waits for me, mockingly, at the top of the stairs.

I open the lid to the washing machine and the stale smell of damp clothes hits me. I forgot to put that load in the dryer yesterday. There was more than enough going on to distract me from completing that simple task. Now I have to wash it again, forcing the pileup of laundry to grow like cars in a traffic jam.

Opening my laptop, I'm greeted by business e-mails. Deadlines, commitments, requests, dream opportunities. All good stuff. All things I'm excited about, honored by. And all things that leave me wondering if I'm good *enough*. I think about one particular dream, that one that seems so far-fetched and yet is becoming increasingly more within reach. There is no way that I have *enough* of what it takes to make that dream a reality.

> What would it be like to be quieted by His love? To feel Him rejoicing over me with gladness?

Hopping to my personal e-mails, the onslaught continues. Field trips, volunteering, church commitments, swim meet schedule, basketball practice schedule, fund-raisers. Is there *enough* of us to go around? I scan through them, trying to decide what I can weed out before my exhausted husband sees them. He's overwhelmed already, and I long to spare him from becoming even more so. Am I doing *enough* to help him? I start to make a grocery list, willing myself to remember the things I supposedly made mental notes of throughout the week. I'm quite certain I will still leave the store without much-needed items that I won't realize I forgot to buy until I've already reached home. And suddenly it's all too much.

I sit at my kitchen table, everything running through my head. The

needle on the record player in my mind is stuck on the
same phrase. *You're not enough, you're not enough, you're
not enough, you're not enough.* **I** know it's not true. I
think I know it's not true. I should know it's not true,
right? But somewhere between *knowing* it and *feeling* it
there seems to be a breakdown. I'm becoming more and

more convinced that this breakdown comes as a result of my doubt. In the
quiet moments, in the darkness, in the recesses of my heart, I doubt that God
truly loves me just as I am. That He wants me to come to Him and just "be."
That He doesn't have a list of requirements and expectations waiting for me.
That I am *enough* for Him. Even simply uttering those words is difficult. And
yet, His letter to me tells me the truth. Reveals just how wrong I am. *"The
Lord your God is in your midst, a mighty one who will save; he will rejoice over
you with gladness; he will quiet you by his love; he will exult over you with loud
singing"* (Zephaniah 3:17 esv).

What would it be like to be quieted by His love? To feel Him rejoicing
over me with gladness? I want to tell you I know that feeling. But if I'm being
honest, I'm not sure I have ever really, truly allowed Him to do that for me.
But lately, I have felt a change coming over my heart. Slowly, very slowly, I'm
coming to realize two things. The first is that *I'm not enough.* And the second
is that *I am enough.* Confused yet? Well, you see, there's an interesting dichotomy that occurs when we embrace the truth of His love.

On the one hand, we are made aware of the fact that without Him, we
are nothing. Have nothing. *"I am the vine; you are the branches. If you remain
in me and I in you, you will bear much fruit; apart from me you can do nothing"*
(John 15:5). Totally shallow, emptied, nothing. Like branches split from a
tree during a storm and lying on the ground. They will not continue to grow
and flourish without being connected to the roots, to the vine.

So we have to come to that place where we recognize our deep need for Him. A need that was created by Him and can only be filled by Him. We aren't enough. We, on our own, aren't enough. But He is! He is enough for us. There's another hand, though. The piece that makes it such a dichotomy. Because, at the same time, He tells us that, in fact, we *are* enough. We are loved and cherished. We were worth the sacrifice of His Son. He exults over us.

> *Then Christ will make his home in your hearts as you trust in him. Your roots will grow down into God's love and keep you strong. And may you have the power to understand, as all God's people should, how wide, how long, how high, and how deep his love is. May you experience the love of Christ, though it is too great to understand fully. Then you will be made complete with all the fullness of life and power that comes from God.* (Ephesians 3:17–19 NLT)

We are able to come to Him, just as we are, and simply receive.

This dichotomy, this two sides of the grace coin, is a mystery that I haven't fully come to understand. I honestly don't know that I ever will. I am broken and yet made whole in Him. I am empty and yet filled by Him. I am a mess and yet beautiful to Him.

And that is enough.

The leaves are beginning to
turn and your home will be
filled with the fragrance of
fall while this delicious snack
is roasting in the oven.

ROASTED HAZELNUTS

INGREDIENTS

_ fresh hazelnuts*

_ 2 Tbs. olive oil

_ 2 Tbs. honey

_ 2 tsp. sea salt

_ 1 tsp. pepper

_ 1½ tsp. paprika

_ 1 tsp. celery salt

_ 1½ tsp. ground cumin

INSTRUCTIONS

*If hazelnuts are still in the skin, roast at 400° F for 10 minutes on a parchment-lined baking sheet. Remove from oven and wrap in a kitchen towel to allow them to steam and skin to loosen. Then roll the towel back and forth working the hazelnuts around to remove the skins.

Once most of the skins are removed, lower oven temperature to 350° F.

Place hazelnuts in a bowl and drizzle with olive oil and honey. Add the salt and other spices, and mix well to evenly coat the nuts.

Pour the mixture back onto the parchment-lined baking sheet.

Roast on the middle rack for 10–15 minutes, stirring regularly so that it browns evenly.

Remove from oven and allow them to cool before eating. Store in an airtight container.

BROKEN
THINGS

- -

*I*t was a glorious day in October. You know all those poems about the beauty of autumn? Well, I'm pretty sure they were written about this particular day. After spending most of the morning in front of the computer, I decided the call to get out of the house was just too loud to ignore. I also decided I would trade in my uniform of yoga pants and old sweatshirt for a cute fall outfit. I topped my favorite jeans with a soft sweater before I turned my attention to footwear options. I caught a glimpse of animal print peeking through a plastic shoe box and I realized it had been months since I last wore those fabulous ballet-style shoes with the little black bows on top. On they went and soon I was practically skipping out the door. With the sunroof open, as I drove through town I could see the vibrant red of the maple trees and bright yellow of the chestnuts glowing against the clear blue sky. The cool breeze perked me up, and I turned up the radio so that I could sing along to my favorite '80s tunes.

I decided to pop into one of my favorite home-décor stores and was soon happily wandering the aisles on the lookout for just the right pieces. As I meandered, I began to notice a strange sound that seemed to be following closely behind me. It took a few minutes before I realized this sound was actually coming from me! Or, more accurately, it was coming from my shoe. I looked down and noticed that the entire sole was coming off and my animal-print ballet slipper was turning into a flip-flop. Now, in that moment, I had a decision to make. I could leave my cart full of items sitting there and flip-flop my way right out of the store, or I could figure out a solution to my problem. If it hadn't been for the fact that I had finally found the perfect duvet cover I might have chosen the first option. But instead, as inconspicuously as possible, I reached down and just pulled the bottom of the shoe right off. Yes, it made me slightly lopsided and yes, I could pretty much feel the floor through the thin layer of fabric that remained, but hey, at least I was able to make it to the counter and pay for that duvet cover before trying to inconspicuously shuffle my way out the door.

Once inside the safety of my car, I tried to figure out what on earth would have caused my shoe

> Like those cute, broken leopard-print shoes, I've discovered I have a tendency to hold on to my broken parts. . . . While God extends me grace, so often I fail to extend it to myself.

to just fall apart like that. And that's when I remembered. All those months ago, when I had last worn those adorable shoes, I had noticed the sole coming loose a bit. But instead of fixing it, I simply stuck that broken shoe in its designated box in my closet and didn't think about it again until this October day, when I was so certain that I was the epitome of sassy fall style. I had taken out those broken shoes, put them on, and worn them with such certainty. As I sat there holding the sole in my hand, I couldn't help but think about how often I hold on to broken things. That decorative urn might be missing a handle, but I'm sure I can just turn it around and no one will notice. One of the fake gems fell out of that necklace and you can see the glue that held it in place, but hey, why don't I just hang it back up with my other necklaces? The missing gem could turn up!

When I really think about this little idiosyncrasy of mine, I realize that perhaps it's a reflection of something a bit deeper. You see, I'd like to think that when I've asked for forgiveness of my sins or when I've resolved an issue, that I'm able to simply throw them away. Rid my life of them altogether, never to see them again. But just like those cute, broken leopard-print shoes, I've discovered I have a tendency to hold on to my broken parts. Instead of throwing them away, I pack them up and store them on the shelves of my heart. Then I take them out and put them on over and over again. While God extends me grace, so often I fail to extend it to myself.

Isaiah 44:22 says, "I have swept away your offenses like a cloud, your sins like the morning mist. Return to me, for I have redeemed you." Think about that for a minute. Have you ever lay on your back and watched a cloud move across the sky? It shifts and changes before, eventually, it disappears altogether. And that exact cloud will never be seen again. That is precisely what God offers us. He gives us the chance to have our sins, our broken parts, swept away. But the thing is, I have to actually give Him that chance. In the moment of confession, I'm able to receive His mercy and forgiveness. I can feel the power of being cleansed of my sins. And yet I treat that forgiveness like a gift I've been handed, unwrapped, expressed appreciation for, and then turned around and given right back to the Giver. When I hold on to those broken parts, it's like I'm telling God that even though I appreciate the gift, I simply cannot keep it. If I'm to truly experience the gift of God's grace, there's no room for me to grasp at the clouds of my sin as He's trying to sweep them away.

That day, sitting in my car and holding the remains of my cute leopard-print shoes, I was faced with a choice. I could keep the broken part and try to reattach it somehow, knowing there was a good chance it would just break again. Or I could let it go. So I did. I let go of the broken shoe. And just as getting rid of those shoes freed up room in my closet, so does accepting the grace God is offering me free up room in my heart.

THE HARVEST

My friend Shauna is a farmer's wife. Now, before we go any further, take any preconceived perceptions you have of farmers' wives and just throw them away. I have yet to see Shauna standing in front of a barn, wearing an apron and holding a pitchfork. She is beautiful, incredibly stylish, very put together, and one of the nicest, most sincere women you will ever meet. Shauna comes from a long generation of farmers, was raised as a farmer's daughter, and married a farmer who comes from a long generation of farmers. And she embraces this lifestyle with complete grace. She takes lunch to her farmer husband out in the field and keeps dinner warm for him in the oven so that after a long, exhausting day he is greeted by a hot meal. She cans fruit and bakes amazing concoctions and loves nothing more than to look out her kitchen window at the field of crops just beyond. What I have recently come to learn about Shauna, though, is that she is also incredibly knowledgeable about all things farming. She is a wealth of information about their crops, farming equipment, and the business as a whole. I've never listened more intently to someone with such fabulous hair describe the inner workings of a combine.

Shauna and her husband are grass-seed farmers. I will not pretend that I had any clue how you grow grass seed until I met her. Frankly, it wasn't something that I thought about a whole lot, or ever for that matter. But the longer we have known them, the more fascinated I've become by the entire grass-seed-growing process. For example, until recently, I had never heard the term *seed shattering*. In early agriculture, seeds would easily shatter, or become susceptible to being dispersed as soon as they ripened. But thanks to modern advances, seeds are now retained longer, which leads to a more plentiful harvest. And when your crop, your bread and butter, is seeds, you want to retain as many of them as possible.

> It's easy to see how we might become weakened to the point that when the big storms hit, we might just find ourselves shattering.

I was curious to find out more about what exactly it means for a seed to shatter and what causes this to happen. You see, a farmer works incredibly hard to lay the groundwork for the perfect crop. The soil is carefully prepared, the seeds are carefully chosen, and the planting time carefully planned. Each seed is nurtured in the same way. All receive the same attention and care. And yet, once they begin to grow there is so much that is outside the farmer's control. Those sprouts are now exposed to the elements and the whims of the weather. And prior to the technological advances I mentioned earlier, the risk of shattering seeds was always very high. The farmer wants to harvest as many of the seeds as possible, but there are those that just simply don't make it. They shatter, or fall away, from the rest. And I've wondered, what was it about those seeds that kept them from hanging on until it was time to be harvested? What made them different? According to my research, the answer to that is that there are some seeds that just aren't nourished enough, aren't strong enough to make it all the way through the growing season to harvest. I kind of feel sad for those seeds. They held all the same promise, all the same possibility, and yet they came up just short of seeing it fulfilled.

As is my tendency, I like to draw comparisons between the things I learn or experience and my faith journey. So, it comes as no surprise that my seed-shattering education took me to a place of thinking about how we as people are so like those seeds. When we become followers of Christ, we are all given the same opportunity. We're all offered the chance to grow to be more like Him and to share His grace and truth with others. But then we hit the roadblocks. The things in life that tempt us to veer off course. We're forced to confront our sins, we face challenges and difficulties, and we battle our weaknesses. And along the way, it's easy to see how we might become weakened to the point that when the big storms hit, we might just find ourselves shattering. Those storms tempt us to doubt God and His plan for our lives. They challenge everything we've known to be true, and if we aren't staying in His Word and relying on His promises we will struggle to make it to the harvest. I'll admit that when I first began processing this, I was quick to think that it was all of those other "seeds" that were at risk of shattering. Certainly I was a stronger seed than they. But the truth of the matter is, I leave myself wide open all the time to the risk of being shattered. I slip so easily into complacency or I rely on my own strength instead of that of my heavenly Father, the farmer of my soul.

Second Corinthians 9:10–11 says, "Now he who supplies seed to the sower and bread for food will also supply and increase your store of seed and will enlarge the harvest of your righteousness. You will be enriched in every way so that you can be generous on every occasion, and through us your generosity will result in thanksgiving to God." You see, getting to the harvest is our goal. When we've remained rooted in Him throughout our growing season, through the sunshine and the rain, the storms and the droughts, we have been enriched. And the harvest is our opportunity to have all of that come to fruition. It's our chance to take all we've learned throughout that long growing season and harvest it, generously sharing it with others and offering thanks to God.

The changing season
has us turning our
hearts towards home
and this simple craft
reminds us that there
is no place quite like it.

PUMPKIN
"HOME" SIGN

SUPPLIES

_ faux pumpkin

_ "H," "M," and "E" wood
  letters (we used five inch
  tall letters to match the
  height of the pumpkin)

_ fabric scraps
  (colors of your choice)

_ foam brush

_ decoupage glue

_ piece of wood to serve
  to serve as the stand

_ razor blade

_ scissors

_ hot glue or craft glue

DIRECTIONS

1 Cut your fabric scraps into small, narrow pieces with
your scissors.

2 Apply decoupage glue to the first of your wood
letters then place the fabric strips on top, working
your way around the letter and covering any wood
that's showing. (Remember that this doesn't need to
be perfect.)

3 Repeat this step for all of the other letters, then allow
to dry.

4 Once dry, apply another thin layer of decoupage to
the top of the letters and allow to dry.

5 Attach your letters and pumpkin, spelling out the
word "HOME" to your stand using hot glue or craft
glue.

MELAN-FALL-Y

We walked slowly down the hall together, his little hand clutching mine. The noise from the room got louder and louder the closer we got, and the flurry of activity around the doorway was a good indication of just how important this particular room was. He spotted a few of his friends and quickly we were engulfed in the madness known as the first day of kindergarten. His daddy and I passed his younger sister back and forth as we followed him around the room. He sat at his little desk and took out his school supplies, obviously pleased by the fact that he had his very own pencil case. His teacher showed him where to put his Thomas the Tank Engine lunch box, and before we knew what was happening, it was time for the parents to leave. Hurried photos were taken, reminders were given, and tears were blinked back before we turned to go. I knew that the significance of this moment was lost on my son. And that's just as it should be. After all, when you are a six-year-old boy, you are only thinking about how many minutes it will be until you get to eat your snack and run around outside with your buddies.

As we walked toward the parking lot, I caught a glimpse of another class-room. The differences between the two weren't lost on me. There were a few parents hanging around but they didn't stay long. Hugs and kisses were kept to a minimum if there were even present at all, and any tears on the part of the parents would have been met with utter mortification from their child. This was the fifth grade, after all. With my daughter squirming in my arms, I stared at that doorway for a minute and thought about how big those kids looked, how much older. And, on that first day of kindergarten, dropping off my son for his first day of fifth grade seemed eons away. But we all know, that's not true, now, is it? Because, in the blink of an eye, there I was, saying good-bye to my fifth grader on the first day of school and feel-ing far more emotional about it than I did even on that day six years earlier when we had walked through the door to kindergarten.

> Maybe feeling melan-fall-y is actually a gift. A chance to pause and revel in this season before moving on quickly to the next one.

Fall and back-to-school time brings with it such mixed emotions for me. There's all of the excitement that a new school year brings, and frankly, I'm a sucker for the smell of brand-new pen-cils. I love knowing that soon the air will be crisp and I'll be wearing my favor-ite boots and sweaters. We'll be visiting the pumpkin patch and, of course, in the back of our minds we know that Christmas is just around the corner. But there's another feeling that rises to the surface of my heart each year around this time. As my kids head off to begin a new school year, a little bit taller, and all around me I see dramatic and colorful evidence of change, I'm left with an emotion that can only be described as bittersweet. It's a feeling I've lovingly begun referring to as melan-fall-y. Time is moving forward and moving quickly, too quickly, if you ask me. With each leaf that falls I think, *Slow down, slow down.* They reach this climactic moment and then fall to the ground in a pile while what remains above are bare branches. And then it's done. And I know that there will never be another fall quite like this one, or the one last year, or the year before that. I can't stop it all from happening, just like I can't keep my children from growing so quickly by putting books on their heads.

I used to feel so conflicted about this melan-fall-y feeling that arose in me every year. How could I love this season so intensely and yet feel such a sense of sadness inside at the same time? And then I began to look at it in a different way. Perhaps my melan-fall-y wasn't something to be pushed down. Maybe I was just supposed to sit in it. Let it come up all around me, like when my sister and I would bury ourselves in the big pile of leaves our dad had just raked, until only our eyes were visible. Maybe this season isn't just about sweaters and boots and mulled-cider candles and pumpkin-spice lattes.

Maybe feeling melan-fall-y is actually a gift. A chance to pause and revel in this season before moving on quickly to the next one. Maybe walking through the woods, leaves crunching beneath my feet, feeling that ache inside, is supposed to remind me of how *finite* I am so that I can remember just how *infinite* my Creator is. Second Corinthians 4:18 says, "So we fix our eyes not on what is seen, but on what is unseen, since what is seen is temporary, but what is unseen is eternal." Maybe God built that ache right into me so that I would seek Him out. So that I would remember that this world isn't my permanent home.

The truth is that when the leaves fall off, the branches that seem so stark and bare hold new growth inside. New life. Fresh starts. And, like the time passing so quickly and my children getting older and my hair getting grayer, there is absolutely nothing I can do to stop it. I can't control it. Frankly, I don't want to. I want to celebrate each passing season, revel in my children's growth, rejoice that there is such a thing as hair-color kits. So, I choose to embrace my melan-fall-y feelings. I allow room for them in my heart. Not *too* much room. But just enough to keep me keenly aware of just how fleeting this world is and how truly grateful I am for every moment I have in it.

HOSPITALITY

Some teenage girls wait anxiously for the latest issue of *Teen Beat* or *Seventeen* to come in the mail. I was not one of them. Oh no. Instead, every month I eagerly anticipated my mom's latest edition of *Traditional Home*. This could explain why I always felt a tad out of place among my peers. For several years running, the incomparable Dixie Carter was *Traditional Home's* writer in residence, and while I loved seeing the photos of the beautiful homes, what I really looked forward to was the way this genteel Southern lady spoke right to my little Southern California girl heart. Every month she shared her thoughts on life and how we interact with each other. I think it was supposed to be a "Miss Manners" type of series. But I believe that her insights went way beyond understanding which utensils to use in what order at a fancy dinner. And there was one article in particular that has stayed with me for all of these years. In it, Dixie Carter said she believed that the purpose of etiquette is to make others feel comfortable. Think about that for a minute. It's not really about you. It's about them.

I've been thinking a lot about how this definition of etiquette is very similar to the definition of hospitality. Or, at least what I think is the real definition. And as we enter into the season of Thanksgiving, when we are opening our homes to friends and family, I feel it is vital that we understand exactly what hospitality really is. You see, somehow in our culture, we've gotten it all mixed up, and we think that hospitality only has to do with a home. But I don't believe that.

In fact, when you get right down to the core of the meaning of hospitality, it doesn't have *anything* to do with a structure at all. I love creating spaces that are warm and welcoming. I love it when I find the perfect side table buried in the back of a consignment store. Or when I move things around and finally find the best combination of items for the top of my grandmother's china cabinet. But the reality is, having a pretty home isn't really part of hospitality. Neither is hosting fabulous parties, or having the most awesome media room for watching the big game, or perfecting the best recipes.

> I think hospitality is an opportunity to show love. And to show we care.

You see, I think hospitality is actually more a way of being rather than doing. One definition I've read said that hospitality is the "act of caring." And I believe that acts of caring can take place just about anywhere. Yes, it should happen in our homes. But it should also be happening in our everyday interactions. There are opportunities all around us to practice hospitality.

One evening not too long ago, as I sat watching my daughter at swim practice, I heard the telltale sounds of a kid throwing a temper tantrum. I looked over to the younger swimmers and saw a little guy who wanted absolutely nothing to do with the water. He wailed when his mom tried to get him to go in and then he wailed when she threatened to have them leave swim practice. She was in a lose-lose situation, and her child was only getting louder. And everyone was watching. After somehow managing to scoop him up as his arms and legs flailed, she marched past all of us sitting there in the chairs and you could just see it all over her face. *Frustration. Anger. Weariness. Embarrassment.*

She was gone for a while and then came back with her son in a more sub-dued state of mind. But as they got closer to that water, he went right back to wailing and flailing. This precious mom scooped him up *again* and marched in front of all of us *again,* looking even more weary and embarrassed. This time, though, as she was getting ready to pass by me, I reached out my hand to gently touch her arm and just said, "It's okay. We've all been there." And as her son continued to wail and flail, she looked at me with the most grateful eyes and the embarrassment that I had seen on her face earlier was now gone. We shared a chuckle together and then she hurried right on out of there. It was a simple moment. Probably no one else noticed. But I like to think that in those five seconds of interaction, that worn-out mom experienced an act of caring. At least I hope she did.

Dixie Carter said that the purpose of etiquette is to make others feel comfortable. And while I think that hospitality is also about making others feel comfortable, I believe that it goes far beyond that. I think hospitality is an opportunity to show love. And to show we care. Once again, it's about them, not about us. For some of us, extending ourselves in this way comes naturally. But for others it just feels so awkward and uncomfortable. I mean, are we really all supposed to have the "gift" of hospitality? Well, yes. Yes, we are. First Peter 4:9 says we are to "Show hospitality to one another without grumbling" (ESV). Wow! It doesn't get much

more blunt than that, does it? But here's the good news. Learning manners is a process, right? I mean, anyone who's raised kids knows that teaching them not to chew with their mouths open or remember to put the toilet seat down or remember to actually flush the toilet or to say please and thank you or to wipe their mouths on a napkin instead of their sleeve (not that any of these things happen in *my* house!), knows that it is an ongoing, daily effort. So, doesn't it stand to reason that learning to be more hospitable would be a process too? We tell our kids all the time that the most important thing to us is that they are trying and that we can see evidence of their efforts. No one gets *all* of it right *all* of the time. But it's the effort that's put into something that really matters. Whether that something is learning if the bread plate is supposed to go on your right or your left or learning how to extend love and care to those around you.

In his book *The Hospitality Commands*, Alexander Strauch said, "Hospitality, therefore, is a concrete, down-to-earth test of our fervent love for God and His people. Love can be an abstract, indistinct idea; hospitality is specific and tangible. We seldom complain about loving others too much, but we do complain about the inconveniences of hospitality. Hospitality is love in action. Hospitality is the flesh and muscle on the bones of love. Through caring acts of hospitality, the reality of our love is tested."

I think even Dixie Carter would agree with that, don't you?

Words of gratitude and thanksgiving written on chalkboard tags at each place setting will be a blessing to all who gather at your table this season.

CHALKBOARD
LEAF NAPKIN RINGS

SUPPLIES

_ empty cardboard toilet
paper tubes
_ burlap
_ wood leaf cutouts
_ chalkboard paint
_ hot glue gun
_ chalk

INSTRUCTIONS

1 Cut the toilet paper tubes in half (one tube will make two napkin rings).

2 Cut a length of burlap to be able to fit around the tube, completely covering it.

3 Then, wrap the burlap around the tube and secure with hot glue.

4 Paint the leaf cutouts with the chalkboard paint and let dry before applying a second coat for optimum coverage.

5 Once dry, write out inspiring words of your choice in chalk.

6 Attach the leaves to the burlap-covered ring with hot glue, or if the leaves come with a pre-punched hole (like the ones pictured) then tie onto the ring with twine.

7 Slip napkins inside and enjoy customizing them to any holiday.

MIND THE GAP

From the moment I read the first lines of Jane Austen's *Pride and Prejudice* I just knew there was a good chance that I was actually meant to be British. I'm pretty sure that somewhere along the line things got off track because I ended up being born in Ohio instead. In my mind, though, I should have been strolling along cobblestone streets, having tea with Mr. Darcy, or feverishly scribbling down my every thought onto the pages of a leather-bound journal by candlelight. You can imagine my absolute delight, then, when my husband and I had the opportunity to travel to the United Kingdom in the fall of 2002. It was like the mother ship was calling me home. If the mother ship served cucumber sandwiches with the crusts cut off.

I'm not quite sure what I expected when we landed at Heathrow Airport on that cold and wet October day. It's fair to say that in the back of my mind, I might have envisioned being picked up by a horse-drawn carriage and whisked away to a manor house in the countryside. Instead, upon our arrival in London, we were quickly swallowed up by the masses heading toward the underground rail system. Not only were we completely overwhelmed as we attempted to determine exactly which train we were supposed to board, but we were also aware that our extremely sleep-deprived state could cause us to end up heading in the absolute wrong direction. Miraculously, we managed to locate the right line on the map and after making our way toward our train, we waited for it to arrive. Our modern-day chariot came roaring into the station and somehow, like salmon swimming upstream, we were able to board, but not before I heard a booming voice overhead issue a warning: "MIND THE GAP!" Honestly, I didn't think much about it at the time, because I was solely focused on not getting separated from my husband or my luggage while being jostled this way and that. But from that point on, every time we boarded a train we heard the same announcement. Over and over and over we were told to mind the gap. This little space between the platform and the doors of the train was obviously pretty important. It kind of made us confused. I mean, it was such a small gap. My husband and I hadn't even noticed

> When we don't tend to all areas of our faith, we leave ourselves wide open for gaps to develop. It's in the gaps where we find we are the most vulnerable to sin and temptation.

it when we boarded that first train. Did people really need to be reminded to lift their feet to the appropriate height so as to not trip as they transitioned from platform to train? Apparently so!

We joked about minding the gap throughout our travels across England and Scotland. And then, as we went to board the train in Edinburgh to head back to London, it happened. My suitcase got stuck as I was rolling it off the platform. The wheels were wedged into that sliver of space known to everyone as the gap. Obviously I hadn't fully appreciated the warnings I'd been given. I tugged my suitcase free and made it onto the train just as the doors were closing. It struck me that the gap hadn't seemed like that big of a deal until it was, in fact, a big deal. Until the wheels of my suitcase were stuck in that gap, I was happy not to give it a second thought. I had become careless about minding the gap and I paid the price.

I've always thought of myself as someone who is fairly self-aware. But just like that space between the train and the station platform, I find there are times when I'm not mindful of the gaps in my faith. It's easy to think I can decide which areas are worthy of my focus and which aren't. Second Peter 1:5–8 says,

For this very reason, make every effort to add to your faith goodness; and to goodness, knowledge; and to knowledge, self-control; and to self-control, perseverance; and to perseverance, godliness; and to godliness, mutual affection; and to mutual affection, love. For if you possess these qualities in increasing measure, they will keep you from being ineffective and unproductive in your knowledge of our Lord Jesus Christ.

Those gaps at the train station seemed so harmless and tame but they held hidden dangers. I'm thinking that stuck suitcase wheels were a minor inconvenience compared to getting the wheels of a stroller stuck while a child is strapped into the seat. When we don't tend to all areas of our faith, we leave ourselves wide open for gaps to develop. It's in the gaps where we find we are the most vulnerable to sin and temptation. I heard those warnings being shouted at me over the loudspeaker at the train station but after awhile they just became background noise. Making the effort to add to our faith means that we are minding the gaps, aware of the areas that we tend to ignore. Maybe there is sin we've just become so comfortable with that we don't even recognize it anymore. Or maybe we have simply grown lazy in our pursuit of a deeper relationship with Christ. We've forgotten what it felt like when we experienced those first glorious moments of salvation, when the muck and the mire of our sin was washed away by the cleansing waters of forgiveness and grace.

Among the lesser-known works of Jane Austen is this prayer: "Thou art everywhere present, from Thee no secret can be hid. May the knowledge of this, teach us to fix our thoughts on Thee, with reverence and devotion that we pray not in vain." Leave it to Jane to know the solution to avoiding complacency. When we fix our thoughts on Him and humbly ask that He reveal the gaps in our faith, we are able to see them for what they really are. Those gaps are opportunities. They provide us with the chance to grow and strengthen our relationship with our Savior. And a chance for adding deeper layers to our faith, if only we will mind the gaps.

HOME

● ●

*Y*ou know we call it the 'coast' and not the 'beach,' right?" It was 1996 and my boyfriend was attempting to give me a brief linguistics lesson while we visited his family in Oregon over winter break. He was eager to show me around his hometown and take me for a drive along the "coast." I was a Southern California girl, and frankly, this slight nuance in terminology was lost on me. Besides, I was in love and not really paying much attention. He could have told me they called it the "watering hole" and I would have simply nodded and gone along with it.

But as we wound our way west, I realized that this was nothing like the Pacific Coast Highway I was used to. Not only were we passing farms and forests, but the landscape gave no indication that we were near anything even remotely coastal. Nowhere in California did I have to pass a lumber mill to see the ocean! As we came up over a hill, suddenly there it was. It was so wonderfully familiar and yet totally foreign at the same time.

This version was like nothing I had seen before, and I realized why my boyfriend had tried to prepare me. The waves crashed against jagged rocks, and the only patches of sand I saw looked anything but warm and welcoming. Wind whipped around us as we stood at the edge of a cliff to try to capture the moment on film. I felt less like a Valley Girl and more like a character out of a Brontë novel! Then and there I decided that this "coast" was not for me. How could anyone find this appealing?

Three years later, I found myself leaving behind my beloved beaches of Southern California and following that former boyfriend, now husband, to Oregon. Our new residence was only an hour from the coast. But moving in the middle of a cold and rainy winter did not make me inclined to give it another chance. Needless to say, I was suffering from a bit of culture shock.

And while I might have had a lovely structure to live in with my new husband, I couldn't help but feel an acute awareness that this was not my home.

> Only He can provide us with the kind of peace, security, and rest that will make us feel at home no matter where we are or what challenges we face.

Growing up in the church, I often heard the phrase "God-shaped hole" to describe that deep longing and desire we have built into us that can only be fulfilled through a personal relationship with Christ. But I also believe that each of us has a home-shaped hole. And just like that God-shaped hole, I think that our home-shaped hole is put there on purpose. We all have the need for a place to belong. A place where we are known. A place where we can really be ourselves. But for some of us, the pursuit of home has been met with challenges. Maybe you, like me, have moved around a lot. Or maybe the only representation you had of home was one that was anything but a safe and secure haven.

Isaiah 32:18 says, "My people will live in peaceful dwelling places, in secure homes, in undisturbed places of rest." God's desire is for us to experience peace, security, and rest. But I believe that in this particular passage of scripture, He isn't necessarily referring to physical structure. Our longing for home, the longing that He built right into us, is really a longing for Him. When I think about home, I think of a place to know and be known. And as we pursue knowing our heavenly Father on deeper and deeper levels, we get to feel that overwhelming sense of security that comes from really and truly being known. Known for all of our strengths and all of our flaws and loved anyway. Only He can provide us with the kind of peace, security, and rest that will make us feel at home no matter where we are or what challenges we face.

During those long, rainy first few months in Oregon, I realized that I needed to change my definition of home. And my ache for what I thought I needed to find here on earth, slowly became an ache for a different kind of home. It was an ache for something that was outside of myself but could not be bound by time and space. An ache for the deepest sense of belonging I could possibly imagine. And the more I released my need to find security in a physical home, the more I was able to embrace the truth that my home-shaped hole could only be filled by the Master Builder.

Eventually, the winter months gave way to spring and with it the most glorious shades of green I had ever seen. That rain has to be good for something, right? As the days grew longer and I began to thaw out, my husband asked me if I would like to take a drive along the coast. Perhaps I was feeling homesick for the ocean. Or perhaps in my heart I knew I needed to fully embrace my new surroundings. We hopped in the car and headed west, past those same farms, forest, and lumber mill. While we drove, we reminisced about that day, years before, when as boyfriend and girlfriend we had set out along the same route. And, before I knew it, I felt a stirring in my heart. This road and I had history. It had seen that boyfriend and girlfriend filled with love, hopes, and dreams for the future. And now it was seeing that same young couple turned husband and wife making those dreams a reality.

We came up over the hill and, once again, I was startled. Only this time it was by the beauty that stretched out before me. The sun peeking through the clouds created a glistening effect on the water as the tide rolled in and out. On one side of the winding road, dense evergreens rose up like giants. And on the other side the infinite expanse of the ocean reminded me of just how small and finite I really am. This was the coast. And I was home.

The perfect combination
of sweet and tart, this cider
recipe tastes like a slice of
apple pie in a mug!

APPLE PIE CIDER

INGREDIENTS

_ 16-oz. apple juice

_ 1 apple
   *(choose a crisp variety
   such as Red Delicious,
   Fuji, or Honeycrisp)*

_ apple pie spice

_ 4 whole cloves

_ 1 orange

_ 4 cinnamon sticks

INSTRUCTIONS

Slice an apple in 1/4" slices. Sprinkle with apple pie spice and bake on cookie sheet at 280° F for 20 minutes, turning over slices halfway through.

Combine apple juice, cloves, orange slices, and cinnamon sticks in small saucepan. Add ½ tsp. apple pie spice and heat through, stirring occasionally.

Strain cider mixture into mugs and garnish with slice of dried apple.

(Serves 4)

THE
CIDER PRESS

· ·

I watched her as she struggled to put all her weight into turning the heavy wood-and-iron handle. On tiptoes she pushed down on it, willing it to move just a little, as her brow furrowed and her lips pursed in concentration. She seemed to know, instinctively, that if she could get the crank to start turning just a few inches, it would get easier to turn and she would start seeing the results of the pressure she was exerting.

This was one of our favorite fall activities. Visiting the Old Mill, decked out in all its autumn glory. And the most popular attraction was the old-fashioned cider press. We would watch as apple after apple was pushed toward the press and then wait in anticipation to see the amber juice run freely out the other side. Just watching would bring the memory of the sweet, crisp taste of fresh cider to our taste buds. Our children loved getting to be part of the process, if even for just a few turns of the crank, of turning apples to cider.

We would discuss how the best and prettiest apples never made it to the apple cider baskets. Those apples were put out for display, to be chosen for apple munching and apple pie baking. The apples that were too small, too bruised, not quite perfect, those apples were sent off to the press. Pressed hard, pressed out, pressed to squeeze every last bit of juice that is the actual life and essence of the apple. They had the goodness pressed from them and the result was sweet and delicious. The apple might not have resembled an apple anymore, by shape or texture, but the best of the apple was poured from the end of the press, ready to be used in a different but equally wonderful way.

By submitting to the pressure and refining, that bruised, too-small, misshapen apple is able to produce a sweetness that quenches the thirst.

How often do you feel like one of those apples making its way through the cider press? Maybe you are feeling bruised and small and unworthy, and moving through life in a way you didn't imagine for yourself. The pressures of life begin to build, and you wonder what you did to end up where you are, with all sides seeming to close in on you.

> Submitting to the pressure with a glad heart, and allowing it to refine you, will bring forth the sweetness of Christ in you.

This is where Paul found himself, as he traveled through Asia spreading the gospel to the early church. He writes to the church of Corinth, "We do not want you to be uninformed, brothers and sisters, about the troubles we experienced in the province of Asia. We were under great pressure, far beyond our ability to endure, so that we despaired of life itself" (2 Corinthians 1:8).

Paul found himself under great pressure. Pressure that they found to be far beyond their ability to endure. Maybe that is how you are feeling right at this moment. Under such a great pressure that you may even feel despair of life itself.

You find yourself crying out to God, asking Him to remove this pressure. To remove the pain that is crushing you from all sides. Before you despair, sweet sister, listen to what Paul goes on to say to the Corinthians.

We are hard pressed on every side, but not crushed; perplexed, but not in despair; persecuted, but not abandoned; struck down, but not destroyed. We always carry around in our body the death of Jesus, so that the life of Jesus may also be revealed in our body. For we who are alive are always being given over to death for Jesus' sake, so that his life may also be revealed in our mortal body. So then, death is at work in us, but life is at work in you. (2 Corinthians 4:8–12)

When pressed upon by all sides of this life, what do you produce? We reveal our true nature in how we respond to, and when we are under, pressure. Is Christ revealed in you when you feel crushed and persecuted?

When we feel under the pressure of the trials of this world, we need to remind ourselves that, "greater is he that is in you, than he that is in the world"! (1 John 4:4 KJV). This is a promise!

A promise that Jesus is in you and with you and ready to reveal Himself to you and to those around you, through your trials and tribulations and how you respond to them. Submitting to the pressure with a glad heart, and allowing it to refine you, will bring forth the sweetness of Christ in you. When we truly understand that the pressures from this world can be used to give honor to the Lord and to create a holiness in us, it can change how we react and relate to them and to those around us.

Do you use the pressures at work as an opportunity to show your co-workers *who* is in you? When faced with pressures at home, do you use them as an excuse to lash out at your husband and children? Do you allow the sweetness of Jesus to pour out of you and over your family, or is it a flood of bitterness and resentment?

Jesus made us this promise as well: "Give, and it will be given to you. A good measure, pressed down, shaken together and running over, will be poured into your lap. For with the measure you use, it will be measured to you" (Luke 6:38).

Let's take the good measure, given to us through Jesus Christ, and allow it to be pressed down, so that it runs over into our own lives and into the lives of all we encounter. Let's let them see the sweetness of Christ in us, under all the circumstances and pressures of life, so that they may know where our strength comes from!

Winter

With the approach of Christmas, we find ourselves longing for the warmth and comforts of home. Not only are we celebrating the birth of our Savior, Jesus Christ, in this season, but we are also presented with the opportunity to look back and reflect on the past year and to look forward to what a new year holds. But when the stockings are packed away and the last cookie has been eaten, winter can often feel long, dark, and never ending. We can find ourselves wondering if there will ever be warm days again.

In the winter season of our faith, we often find that God can seem far away, and as we face great difficulties we wonder if we will ever feel the warmth of His love again. This is a time when we have the opportunity to reflect on how far God has brought us and how we can trust in Him to carry us through even the darkest seasons in our lives.

ADVENTURES IN ADVENT

・・・・・・・・・・・・・・・・・・・・・・・・・・・・・・・・・・・・・・

J could see it all so clearly in my mind. The twinkling lights of the Christmas tree in the corner of the room. Perry Como's voice crooning as only he can croon those holiday classics. Snowflakes gently falling outside the window. Steaming cups of hot cocoa with marshmallows, and my family gathered together, perhaps wearing matching holiday pajamas. My husband would take out his Bible and read to us the story of that very first Christmas. The kids would be so moved by the moment that they would forever have it emblazoned in their memories. They would pay homage to us years later as they recalled to everyone near and far how their parents, particularly their mother, had created such magical holiday experiences for them. Because I could see all of this playing out so clearly in my mind, I just knew that I could turn this vision into a reality. I informed my husband that come Sunday evening, we would be making Christmas memories as a family like nobody's business. When I described to him what I envisioned, he just looked at me warily. But there was no room for skepticism in my Advent dream.

Sunday rolled around and after dinner we told the kids that we would be meeting in the family room to do something special. Their little eyes lit up with excitement, and I could see all the pieces of my Advent puzzle falling right into place. I sent my husband to grab his Bible, checked that the Christmas tree lights were turned on, made sure Perry was crooning at just the right volume, and flipped the switch on the gas fireplace. I instructed the kids to sit down on the floor and explained that we were going to start a new tradition together as a family. We were going to celebrate Advent and Daddy was going to read to us the story of the first Christmas, a little bit each Sunday for the four weeks leading up to Christmas, with the last portion to be read on Christmas Eve.

Their lack of reaction gave me my first clue that perhaps this evening wasn't going to go as planned. But just as my husband was opening the Bible, my son yelled, "Wait! Can I read it?" Oh, this was even better than I had imagined! Our child showing so much interest in Advent that he wanted to read the story from the Bible to us himself. I fought back tears as my heart swelled with pride. Without hesitation my husband passed it over to him and showed him where to start reading. He began slowly working his way

> As Mary awaited the arrival of her son, the son who was also her Savior, I've often wondered if she was consumed with thoughts of how different her life was now going to be.

through the verses and then it happened. Someone passed gas. Loudly. Really loudly. And it smelled bad. Really bad. Uncontrollable giggling, the inevitable response, ensued and soon the glow of the fireplace, the twinkling lights of the Christmas tree, and even Perry Como couldn't make up for the fact that my Advent dream was becoming more of a nightmare. We tried to regroup and start over but it was too late. The kids quickly moved from giggling to wiggling to wanting to be anywhere except sitting quietly in some kind of wannabe Hallmark-movie moment.

After tucking them in bed for the night, I returned to the family room and sat staring at those fake logs glowing in my fireplace. I thought about how I had dreamed, had expected, the evening to go. Glancing over at the Bible, which had been casually tossed aside amid all of the gaseousness, I began to think about how often my expectations don't match up with reality. About how I build things up to unrealistic proportions, which so often leave me feeling disappointed, and how after all these years I should know better. I picked up the Bible and began to read about another woman whose dreams for her life didn't quite turn out the way she had planned. A young woman whose expectations for her future were suddenly and drastically altered.

The angel went to her and said, "Greetings, you who are highly favored! The Lord is with you." Mary was greatly troubled at his words and wondered what kind of greeting this might be. But the angel said to her, "Do not be afraid, Mary; you have found favor with God. You will conceive and give birth to a son, and you are to call him Jesus. He will be great and will be called the Son of the Most High. The Lord God will give him the throne of his father David, and he will reign over Jacob's descendants forever; his kingdom will never end." (Luke 1:28–33)

The word *advent* means "arrival or coming" and as Mary awaited the arrival of her son, the son who was also her Savior, I've often wondered if she was consumed with thoughts of how different her life was now going to be. I think that sometimes in our retelling of the Christmas story, we forget that Mary was just a girl. A young girl who had hopes and dreams for her future, ones that up to that point hadn't included giving birth to the King of kings. But, in verse 38 we are given a glimpse, through her response, of how we are to respond when our lives don't go according to our plans. "'I am the Lord's servant,' Mary answered. 'May your word to me be fulfilled'" (Luke 1:38).

I believe that Mary was able to rest in the knowledge that, while everything might not be going according to her plan, the outcome would be far more amazing than she could have possibly imagined. So I choose to embrace my own reality, knowing that while there are so many things that have happened differently than I had planned, they always end up better than anything I could have orchestrated. Hallmark can keep its picture-perfect moments. I'll take my version any day!

Count down the days
until Christmas with
loving reminders of
God's promises which
capture the true heart
of the season.

GOD'S PROMISES ENVELOPE ADVENT CALENDAR

SUPPLIES

_ large wood pallet, piece of wood, beadboard or even an empty frame
_ envelopes and notecards *(color of your choice)*
_ sticker numbers
_ twine or ribbon *(colors of your choice)*
_ pushpins
_ cardstock paper *(color of your choice)*
_ decorative clothespins

INSTRUCTIONS

1 Cut 4 pieces of string to fit across the width of the wood piece or frame.

2 Attach each piece of ribbon to the sides of your board with the pushpins, spacing them evenly apart.

3 Place your sticker numbers on each envelope from 1–24.

4 Print 24 Bible verses about the promises of God and put them inside each envelope.

5 Attach the envelopes with cards inside to the strings with the decorative clothespins.

MY ROAD
LESS TRAVELED

· ·

We went on a lot of road trips growing up. A lot. In fact, I don't think I realized that people took any other kind of vacation until I was much older. I have vivid memories of my mom waking us up in the wee hours of the morning and hustling us out to the Datsun station wagon, where the backseat had already been folded down and sleeping bags and blankets were waiting for us to snuggle into. This was obviously before the days of seat-belt laws. She would have lovingly packed a travel bag for each of us, with plenty of coloring books and crayons and a few new surprises tucked in to help occupy two little girls during those long hours on the road.

Prior to each trip, my dad would spend countless hours poring over maps and charting our course. In another life, I think he would have made an incredible ship captain. One of his greatest pleasures was not only trying to find the best route to our destination but also researching what special attractions we might be able to enjoy along the way. I'm fairly certain I've seen every single historic western town from sea to shining sea. But for all of his meticulous planning, my dad always left room for the spontaneous. He knew that there were some things you just simply couldn't predict from looking at a map. He always made allowances for detours. Some of them were ones that were outside our control, caused by road work or accidents. But some, well, some detours my dad created just for us. We would be driving along when suddenly he would veer off course. He would see a road that looked promising and before we knew what was happening we were venturing into uncharted territory. My dad loved the idea of what Robert Frost called "the one less traveled."

> When they placed our sweet new baby boy in our arms, we realized how much the adoption of this child was a representation on this earth of God's love and sacrifice for us.

But how often in life do we intentionally choose that road? The one that is less traveled. I tend to prefer the well-beaten path, the predictable trail with clear markings and maybe a Starbucks along the way. One is dark and frightening, winding its way along, with overgrown trees blocking the final destination from our view. The other is brightly lit and wide enough for many to walk down it together. There are no stones and branches to step over, only perfectly paved roads with huge neon signs in the distance, pointing us to our goal. Mary's path was certainly one that was less traveled, and I have often wondered what really went through her mind when the angel Gabriel appeared to her declaring, "Do not be afraid, Mary; you have found favor with God. You will conceive and give birth to a son, and you are to call him Jesus. He will be great and will be called the Son of the Most High" (Luke 1:30–32). "How will this be?" (v. 34), she asked. What do you mean? Why are the plans for my life being so drastically altered?

Now I will be different from the rest, set apart, and my path will be one I go down alone.

My own road to motherhood was certainly unlike what I had imagined. But when they placed our sweet new baby boy in our arms, we realized how much the adoption of this child was a representation on this earth of God's love and sacrifice for us. The grief, loss, and sacrifice of one, providing joy, peace, and fulfillment for another. Who would have thought that our pain-filled, doubt-filled, and dimly lit road would lead us to a destination quite as amazing as this! John 1:4 says, "In him was life, and the life was the light of men" (ESV). Do you trust God to light the way down the darkened path before you? The darkness does not understand the light (John 1:5) that shines through it. It wants us to stay scared and to stay put! It doesn't want us to move forward trusting that the light we follow will lead us to an eternal and everlasting hope.

As frightened and confused and overwhelmed as Mary must have been, she chose to take the road less traveled. Not because she knew that there would be a happy and neatly packaged ending, but because she was an obedient follower of the Lord and she trusted Him to be faithful in His promise, "to do immeasurably more than all we ask or imagine, according to his power that is at work within us" (Ephesians 3:20). Her obedience to God brought our Savior to this earth, in the form of an infant, to live among us, be led to His death on the cross, and rise again!

Therefore, since we are surrounded by such a great cloud of witnesses, let us throw off everything that hinders and the sin that so easily entangles. And let us run with perseverance the race marked out for us, fixing our eyes on Jesus, the pioneer and perfecter of faith. For the joy set before him he endured the cross, scorning its shame, and sat down at the right hand of the throne of God. Consider him who endured such opposition from sinners, so that you will not grow weary and lose heart. (Hebrews 12:1–3)

On all those road trips, my dad knew that veering off course wasn't always going to guarantee us a wonderful outcome. He never knew if what would lie at the end of our detour was going to be a beautifully scenic view, a dead end, or maybe even another detour. But what he did know was that it was always worth taking the chance, because, no matter what, it would be an adventure. Will you run with perseverance down that road less traveled? Because God has paved the way with His shed blood for you and will be the light to guide you when you fear you are growing weary and losing heart.

Two roads diverged in a wood and I—
I took the one less traveled by,
And that has made all the difference.

BEING STILL

$\mathcal{J}$ had been feeling it for months. It was nagging at me, coming up in my mind over and over again. And yet, I couldn't put my finger on just what exactly it was. All I knew was that I was supposed to do something. But, frankly, I was so busy doing so many other "somethings" that I didn't have time to really figure out what this particular "something" could be.

One night in early December found me ready to indulge in a nice, long, hot bubble bath. The kids were in bed, I had finished a huge project for work and wrapped what felt like almost a million Christmas presents, and had the post all scheduled for the next day. My husband was happily watching sports and I was so ready for some "me" time. I could feel my muscles beginning to relax as soon as they hit the water and with my glass of wine and my book at my fingertips, I knew that THIS must be the "something" I was supposed to do. And yet, as I sat there soaking, I found myself feeling almost restless. How could that be, though? Kids in bed? Check! Work done? Check! Hot bubble bath? Check! Good book? Check!

Everything was in place for this to be the perfect moment of relaxation. So why didn't I feel relaxed? I put the book down, leaned my head back, and closed my eyes. And that's when I knew. That feeling, that nagging, that "something" I knew I needed wasn't a bath. It was stillness. I could feel it welling up in me. This longing to be still. When was the last you were really, truly quiet and still? I'm not talking about being sprawled out on the couch watching your favorite show. And sleeping doesn't count. No, I'm talking about experiencing a true quieting of your mind.

As I sat there getting pruny in the bathwater, I tried to remember the last time I had experienced that. And I couldn't. But if I was being honest with myself, I was actually kind of scared to experience it. Which, for the sake of full transparency here, must have meant that in my heart of hearts I'd known all along that I needed to be still but had been intention-

> Suddenly, the nagging feeling, that sense that I was supposed to be doing something, was gone. In its place was a calming of my soul and an overwhelming sense of peace, of truth.

ally avoiding it. But why would I avoid being still? That just sounds like all sorts of craziness, right? Well, frankly, I think I was afraid.

You see, I've recently realized that somewhere along the way in my faith journey, my perception of God has been greatly impacted by my perception of . . . well . . . myself. I put a lot of pressure on myself. I have high expectations for myself. And I struggle with feeling that others have high expectations of me. Sometimes it's hard for me to imagine anyone wanting to spend time with me just because I'm me, and not because they need something from me or want me to fulfill a certain role. So when it comes to approaching the throne of my Savior, I've honestly been filled with almost a sense of dread. Rationally, I know that isn't how I'm supposed to feel.

But, for months now (maybe even years!), I've had this underlying feeling that if I allow myself to be still in His presence, I mean really, truly still, that He's going to require something of me. Ask me to do something outrageous. Like go live in a hut somewhere with no electricity or running water. And this underlying fear has kept me from being able to just *be* in His presence. It's kept me from being still. As I sat there in the bathtub, I could feel God asking me to just trust Him in that moment. *Try Me*, He said.

And suddenly the craving for absolute quiet, absolute stillness, was too overwhelming and I couldn't resist it any longer. I closed my eyes and lowered myself in the water until it covered the tops of my ears. All I could hear was the sound of my own breathing. And quiet. Complete and utter quiet.

The stillness enveloped me, wrapped itself around me like a blanket, and I waited. Waited for God to tell me that I needed to be volunteering more at church. Waited for Him to tell me I was falling short of expectations. Waited for Him to tell me that He wanted us to sell all of our belongings and start looking for a hut to live in. But that's not what I heard. What I heard Him saying to me instead was this. *I've missed you. I'm FOR you. I want you to just BE with Me.* And *I want to be with you.*

Suddenly, the nagging feeling, that sense that I was supposed to be doing something, was gone. In its place was a calming of my soul and an overwhelming sense of peace, of truth. Hebrews 4:16 says, "Let us then approach God's throne of grace with confidence, so that we may receive mercy and find grace to help us in our time of need." It doesn't say "Let us approach God's throne with dread because He's going to tell you how horrible you are." It doesn't say, "Let us approach God's throne and be prepared to be told how we aren't living up to expectations and how we really need to be doing a lot more." It doesn't say, "Let us approach God's throne and come away feeling exhausted and overwhelmed by all that we need to change."

No. It says to approach His throne so that you will be given mercy and grace and help. Those were all of the things my soul had been longing for. They had been there all along, just ready for the taking. But my own expectations of myself, along with the expectations I felt others had for me (real or perceived) had kept me from being able to receive those precious gifts there at His throne. There, in that moment, the water gently lapping up over my ears, my hair floating all around me, I felt such a deep sense of relief. Of renewal. Of letting everything go. I felt His mercy washing away my doubts. His grace cleansing me of my sin. His help in accepting that He loves me without condition. And I was just still.

Whether you give it as a gift or keep it for yourself, the fresh smell of peppermint in this body scrub will definitely put you in the holiday spirit.

PEPPERMINT
SUGAR SCRUB

INGREDIENTS
_ granulated sugar
_ peppermint essential oil
_ coconut oil

SUPPLIES
_ mason jar
_ festive ribbon*
_ label*

DIRECTIONS

Follow the instructions on the back of the coconut oil container in order to get it to a liquid form.

Mix together 1 cup granulated sugar, ½ cup coconut oil, and 10–15 drops of peppermint oil. (If you want the scent to be stronger, add more drops.)

Stir well and then package in mason jars.

*If you are going to be giving this as a gift, put a label on the front describing what's inside and tie a ribbon around the jar.

AND THE SOUL
FELT ITS WORTH

· ·

We stood in the hallway outside the third-grade classroom door, afraid to speak to each other, waiting for what felt like an eternity. Behind that closed door, the future of our stage careers was being determined by a room full of nine-year-olds, and the enormity of the moment had rendered us all silent. Or perhaps we just hoped that if we didn't talk, somehow we would manage to hear a snippet of what was happening inside. Only five minutes earlier, I had been sitting at my desk when my teacher announced that our class would be putting on a production of *Mother Goose*. She asked all those interested in playing the lead part to raise their hands. I can't say what exactly possessed me at that moment, but before I realized what was happening, my hand shot up along with those of three others around the room. All eyes turned in my direction, and I instantly regretted my impulsiveness. We were told to go wait in the hallway so the class could vote for the winner without us seeing who voted for whom and thereby avoid any hurt feelings.

As I stood there waiting, I looked at the other girls and wondered how I had gotten myself into this situation. Who was I kidding? I was the new girl, the one without very many friends. The one who simply wanted to fit in and be liked. I was fully aware of how high the odds were stacked against me. Suddenly, we saw the door handle beginning to turn and we knew that this was a defining moment. Only we would have to wait a bit longer. We were ushered back inside and instructed to take our seats before the big announcement was made. I lowered my head and closed my eyes, wishing I could turn back time and not raise my hand. My teacher began by saying that no matter who won the lead part there would be roles for everyone in the production and then I heard these words: "But the winner of the lead role in our class play this year as voted on by the majority of the class is . . . Vanessa!" What? Did she really just say my name? Did the class really vote for me? I couldn't believe my ears and yet all of the faces turned in my direction confirmed it was true. They had voted for me. Me! The newest girl in the class. Not the most popular girl or the one with the best clothes. Me! They had deemed me worthy of the lead part. And as I sat there basking in that moment, I determined to do everything in my power to live up to their expectations.

> We easily confuse our longing for love or our longing for happiness with the longing to know that we are worthy when they are, in fact, very different things.

Weeks later, the big day arrived and as my mom still tells the story to this day, she and my dad had absolutely no idea of the sheer volume of lines I had memorized, when they sat down in the auditorium for my big debut. And not only had I memorized my own lines, but also those of every part in the entire play. I was at the ready to help my classmates if they needed a cue and there had never been a Mother Goose so well prepared. What I wasn't able to express at nine years old, but felt so deeply in my soul, was that the class had taken a risk on me. And I had made it worth it to them.

The need to feel of worth is one that is so deeply embedded in our souls, isn't it? But it's a need we often don't quite know how to express. We easily confuse our longing for love or our longing for happiness with the longing to know that we are worthy when they are, in fact, very different things. One of my favorite Christmas songs is "O Holy Night," and while each word, each lyric is as familiar to me as the back of my hand, there is one line that somehow, until recently, I managed to never really pay much attention to. It says, "Long lay the world, in sin and error pining, / Till He appeared and the soul felt its worth." Think about that for a moment. Our souls are longing to feel their worth. Prior to the arrival of the infant King in Bethlehem, the world waited, pined, engulfed in sin and error. And it was only through His birth, death, and resurrection that our souls would experience their true value, their full worth. Titus 3:4–7 says,

But when the goodness and loving kindness of God our Savior appeared, he saved us, not because of works done by us in righteousness, but according to his own mercy, by the washing of regeneration and renewal of the Holy Spirit, whom he poured out on us richly through Jesus Christ our Savior, so that being justified by his grace we might become heirs according to the hope of eternal life. (ESV)

The world tells us that our worth is based entirely on the external, on what can be seen. We're not measured simply by our existence, but rather by what we can offer. But thousands of years ago, when our Savior was born, we were told something very different. Before He walked among us. Before He performed miracles. Before He challenged the leaders of the day. Before He was betrayed. Before He was sacrificed. Before He rose from the dead. Before all else, He simply appeared. And it was through His lowly, humble, anything-but-royal appearance that our souls were given the opportunity to experience the fullness of their worth. It is only through being in His presence that we are able to feel the full magnitude of our value. Who He is allows us to know, really know, just who we are. We are beloved. We are cherished. We are worth it.

BREATHLESS EXPECTATION

· ·

When I became a mom of two, I entered into a season of what I found to be a new kind of crazy. I had gotten one child all potty trained and sleeping through the night and drinking out of a cup without a lid and giving me a chance to take a shower and go to the bathroom by myself most of the time. And then, there I was, starting the process all over again. Didn't we just do this?

I vividly remember how I felt in that particular season when I would somehow, magically, find that I had an hour or two all to myself without the munchkins around. I'm pretty sure that the buildup moms feel as they wait for those kid-free moments is exactly like the buildup the astronauts feel as they prepare for the space shuttle to launch. Watching the clock as the minutes, then seconds, count down. Hearts pumping with eager anticipation. Doing all of the last-minute checks to make certain that things will go off without a hitch. And then, it's time. A dramatic pause, maybe a few tears, sparks flying, and then it's all systems go! There was always this glorious moment when I finally found myself alone, when I would simply pause and soak in the silence. I would close my eyes and just feel it enveloping me, wrapping me up and reminding me that I was, in fact, an actual person and not just a pacifier-finding, train-track-building, baby-food-making, diaper-changing robot.

But then, sometimes, that same wonderful silence would become almost overwhelming. I would feel like it was mocking me with all of its possibilities. I'd been craving this alone time and now, all of a sudden I felt a sense of panic beginning to rise up in me. *Should I take a nap? Should I sit down and read a book, which would inevitably lead to taking a nap? Should I clean the kitchen? Should I take a nap? Should I catch up on the shows I haven't watched in two years? Should I take a nap? Should I call that friend I never get to talk to without being interrupted a million times? Should I take a nap?* The thoughts would swirl and twirl in my mind until I felt like I was developing a temporary case of schizophrenia. I would find myself wandering around the house, never actually determining how I was going to spend the time. Here I had longed for, intensely *craved*, a few minutes to myself

> I find myself completely overwhelmed by all the options and stressed out thinking about how critical it is that I make the absolute most out of every day.

and now that I had it, I didn't know what to do with it. What felt like a gift had suddenly become an overwhelming burden because I was so afraid of not making the absolute, positive *most* out of every single minute.

Think about the pressure I was putting on those two hours. They were expected to live up to this fantasy I had created in my mind and somehow magically fulfill every longing. And, inevitably, I would be left feeling let down. The kids would come back home, and my life as mom/pacifier finder/

train track builder/diaper changer/robot would resume and I would look back on that free time with regret.

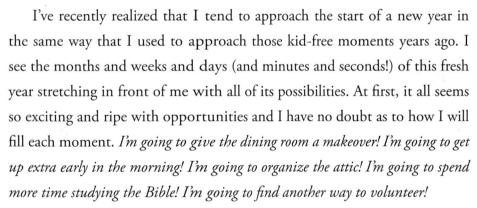

Somewhere deep in the recesses of my heart I knew that I had wasted it. I felt as though I had failed at yet one more thing. As a mom of young children, that sense of failure was already something I was very familiar with. It seemed like at every corner I was coming up short, and now I realized that I was even a failure at what should be a guarantee. I should know how to relax, right? I should know how to make the most of two hours without running around like a chicken with my head cut off. I should feel refreshed afterward, not sad and confused. Shouldn't I?

I've recently realized that I tend to approach the start of a new year in the same way that I used to approach those kid-free moments years ago. I see the months and weeks and days (and minutes and seconds!) of this fresh year stretching in front of me with all of its possibilities. At first, it all seems so exciting and ripe with opportunities and I have no doubt as to how I will fill each moment. *I'm going to give the dining room a makeover! I'm going to get up extra early in the morning! I'm going to organize the attic! I'm going to spend more time studying the Bible! I'm going to find another way to volunteer!*

Then, just like in those days of early motherhood, I find myself completely overwhelmed by all the options and stressed out thinking about how critical it is that I make the absolute most out of every day. Oswald Chambers said,

Certainty is the mark of the commonsense life—gracious uncertainty is the mark of the spiritual life. To be certain of God means that we are uncertain in all our ways, not knowing what tomorrow may bring. This is generally expressed with a sigh of sadness, but it should be an expression of breathless expectation. We are uncertain of the next step, but we are certain of God. As soon as we abandon ourselves to God and do the task He has placed closest to us, He begins to fill our lives with surprises.

You see, I think I've had it all backward. I've spent way too much time trying to be certain of myself and of "all of my ways." And this striving for certainty in my life has led me to that place where the thought of what "tomorrow may bring" doesn't just fill me with a "sigh of sadness." It fills me with fear and doubt. The more I've reached for certainty on my own, the more uncertain and untrusting I've become of God. Frankly, the thought of abandoning myself to Him seems completely and utterly terrifying. The unknown has never been something I've been particularly fond of.

When I was given the glorious gift of kid-free moments all those years ago, it was my inability to abandon myself that ultimately led to it feeling like more a punishment than a blessing. And it always ended with a "sigh of sadness." Not because it was over, but because it never lived up to what I had imagined in my head. But what if I did it differently this year? What if, instead of running around trying to figure out what is going to happen in the months, weeks, days, minutes, and seconds of the new year, I embraced the uncertainty of it all? In fact, what if I not only embraced the uncertainty of it, but I replaced that uncertainty about what tomorrow will bring with certainty about God. About who He is. About His character. About His love for me.

Being certain about God doesn't mean I can't have dreams or make plans or wonder about what is to come. But it does mean that my trust in Him trumps my need for certainty. And I'm ready. I'm ready to abandon myself to Him and to the task He has placed closest to me. I'm ready for my life to be filled with surprises. Which is saying a lot for a girl who absolutely hates surprises! But I know that His surprises will far surpass anything that I could have ever imagined. They always have!

Bring nature indoors by nestling these sweet book page bird ornaments in your tree. An easy project for even the littlest crafter in the family.

BOOK PAGE
BIRD ORNAMENTS

SUPPLIES

_ unfinished wood craft birds
   (found at craft stores)
_ miniature bird nests
   (found at craft stores)
_ book pages
_ twine
_ Mod Podge craft glue
_ glue gun with low-temperature glue stick
_ clear glitter
_ foam paintbrush
_ scissors
_ pencil

DIRECTIONS

1   Trace bird shape onto book pages, using wooden birds as template.

2   Carefully cut out bird to fit onto craft piece. Then, repeat for the other side.

3   Using foam craft brush, brush Mod Podge glue onto one side of the wooden bird and adhere the book page bird onto it.

4   Brush top of book page with light coat of glue and sprinkle with clear glitter, if desired.

5   Allow to dry completely. Then, repeat on the other side.

6   Secure bird into nest with a small amount of low-temperature glue with hot glue gun.

7   Attach a small piece of twine to each side of the nest for hanging.

NEVER-FAILING
LOVE

had been having one of those days with my kids. I don't really want to name any names. But it was mostly the oldest one. After several repetitions of "Please stop doing that" and "Leave your sister alone" and "Don't make me come up there," my patience level was on the edge. And then it was just tipped right over that edge. I don't remember the specifics, but I know it had something to do with someone getting in someone else's face and then someone not telling the truth and then someone tattling and then . . . well . . . you get the idea! Everyone was immediately sent to their respective rooms while I attempted to get back to the Valentine's Day craft I had been trying to work on prior to the countless interruptions. A sweet little craft that represented love. But I wasn't feeling very loving. And I realized that if you are going to make a Valentine's Day craft about love, you probably shouldn't have just lost your patience with your children.

Patience is something I've always struggled with. I think it has a lot to do with the fact that I have always had high expectations for just about everything and everyone in my life. I would put a completely unreasonable amount of pressure on holidays and events, and when they didn't match the picture I imagined in my head, I would feel such a deep sense of disappointment. If you are going to make a craft reflecting a season of love, there should be nothing but loving interactions happening all around you, right? After putting everyone else in time-out, I decided I could use a time-out of my own. I sat down at the kitchen table, grabbed my Bible, and read through 1 Corinthians 13. "Love is patient." Am I? "Love is kind." Do I always show kindness? And not just on the outside but in my heart too? "It does not envy, it does not boast, it is not proud" (v. 4). Ouch!

Here's the thing about the gift of God's love. There is absolutely no pressure, no expectation when it comes to receiving it.

Maybe I don't like this craft after all. I think this is what is known as divine timing! This simple little Valentine's Day craft had stopped me in my tracks. We all know that the flowers and candy and lingerie (which, of course, isn't actually a gift for *me*) aren't really what love is all about. We know that it means so much more. But what about the definitions the Bible presents about love? Is this what comes to mind when we think about love? "It does not dishonor others, it is not self-seeking, it is not easily angered, it keeps no record of wrongs. Love does not delight in evil but rejoices with the truth" (1 Corinthians 13:5–6). I'm thinking the flowers and candy and yes, even the lingerie, sound a whole lot simpler than this definition of love. And then I got to this verse in 1 Corinthians 13. "It always protects, always trusts, always hopes, always perseveres" (v. 7). It sounds so strong. Courageous even! And it made me think about just how much courage it really does take to give love. And how much more courage

it takes to receive love. I've always found that giving love comes easier to me than receiving it. It may have something to do with the fact that I've never quite known how to be on the receiving end of a present. I sit there awkwardly as all eyes are on me, waiting in anticipation as I fumble with the wrapping paper and make jokes to try to distract everyone from my utter lack of gift-receiving social skills. I feel so much pressure to show just the right reaction at just the right time and always think that I've fallen short of what is expected of me. Part of my difficulty comes from this place of feeling completely unworthy of receiving gifts. And I'm fairly certain that this feeling directly correlates with how unworthy I feel to receive the gift of God's love.

As I continued reading through 1 Corinthians 13, I was particularly struck by verse 8: "Love never fails." Never? But I fail. I fail in this kind of loving. I might get some of it right some of the time, but I don't get all of it right all of the time—that is for sure! Then again, I'm going to fail, right? I'm human. I'm going to lose my patience and get angry and be envious and prideful and all of those things. But maybe this verse wasn't just written to instruct me in how to love. Maybe it was also written to remind me of the One who truly does never fail! Because here's the thing about the gift of God's love. There is absolutely no pressure, no expectation when it comes to receiving it. No one watching with anticipation to see if you give the appropriate reaction upon opening it. It's so hard for me to fully grasp the magnitude of a love that never fails. That means it will never disappoint. Never let me down. And even when I'm the one who fails, the amount of love I'm given doesn't decrease. It isn't about whether or not I'm worthy. Because I'm not. None of us are. The gift of God's love to us through the sacrifice of His son, Jesus Christ, isn't about worthiness. It's about love. We are worth that sacrifice not because of who we are, but because of who He is. Our Creator. The One whose love never fails.

So, the next time I hear someone tattling about how someone else did something to annoy the other someone, I'll just look over at my sweet Valentine's Day craft sitting there on my kitchen counter and know that it serves as a very special reminder. A reminder of the day when I truly understood that while I may never live up to the ultimate standard of love, I am grateful to be loved by the One who set the standard in the first place.

IN THE DOLDRUMS

*H*ave you ever wondered where different sayings come from? My son received a really cool game for Christmas, called Word Teasers. Now, in the spirit of complete honesty let me clarify that his parents thought it fell in the "cool" category, while he thought it fell in the "educational" category and those two categories don't always cross over in a twelve-year-old's world. The game gives the background on all of those sayings, or idioms, that have become part of our everyday conversations. Like "raining cats and dogs," "off the cuff," or "penny for your thoughts." The day after Christmas, I somewhat absentmindedly picked up the box of cards and began thumbing through them. It was fascinating to learn just how these phrases I use all the time really originated. Did you know that the phrase "chip on your shoulder" comes from the early 1800s, when a young boy would put a chip of wood on his shoulder and then dare another boy to knock it off? If the second boy did knock it off, then the two boys would fight each other. Or that to "read the riot

act" comes from England, where the police were required to read a procla-
mation known as the Riot Act before they could break up a demonstration
and arrest a crowd?

As I went through the cards in the box of Word Teasers, one particular
phrase caught my eye: "In the doldrums." It's a saying I've used countless
times, and while I've always known that it had something to do with feeling
down or depressed, I've never known how that phrase actually got its start.
You see, years ago, sailors noticed the stillness of the air when they got near
the equator. They named this area "doldrums." Frequently, there is no wind
in this area for weeks on end, and as a result, a ship caught in the doldrums
can end up stranded. They would find themselves stuck. A sailboat isn't going to get very far without at least a little bit of wind. After reading
this I immediately felt myself un-
derstanding just how those sailors
must have felt being caught in the
doldrums.

> The times of silence, or doldrums, in our faith don't mean that we are being punished or that we are just supposed to sit tight until the plan is finally revealed. "God's silences are actually His answers."

So often we find ourselves in
a place where we feel as though
we've been stranded. We're stuck.
Not even the slightest hint of a
breeze or a ripple on the water.
That place, that doldrum, can feel
like the loneliest place on earth. Maybe it's that so often stillness has a best
friend that usually comes along with it. Its name is silence. And silence is
something I'm not all that comfortable with. There have been many seasons in
my life when I have found myself simply staying afloat. I couldn't even chart
a course if I wanted to, because there was no wind to carry me anywhere. In

those seasons I find myself questioning God's silence. The waiting, the inactivity, can feel like some sort of punishment. Waiting isn't something I do with patience. Instead, I find myself almost frenetically trying to figure out what's going to happen next. What's going to happen? When will it happen? How will I know if it's the thing that's supposed to happen? When I find myself in the doldrums, all I'm usually doing is looking for a way out.

But what if we are supposed to look at the doldrums differently? What if instead of watching and waiting for that breeze to come and carry us out of it, we are simply supposed to just float? In his book *My Utmost for His Highest*, Oswald Chambers talks about how we should really approach the seasons of silence. He says,

> *Has God trusted you with His silence—a silence that has great meaning? God's silences are actually His answers. . . . Can God trust you like that, or are you still asking Him for a visible answer? . . . When you cannot hear God you will find that He has trusted you in the most intimate way possible—with absolute silence, not a silence of despair, but one of pleasure, because He saw that you could withstand an even bigger revelation. If God has given you a silence, then praise Him—He is bringing you into the mainstream of His purposes.*

Do you hear that? The times of silence, or doldrums, in our faith don't mean that we are being punished or that we are just supposed to sit tight until the plan is finally revealed. "God's silences are actually His answers." There might not be a wave in sight for miles, but when you are sitting there in that boat, in the doldrums, you are still floating, right? Your boat isn't sinking!

And think about what it means to have God trust us with His silence. It's like He's giving us a gift. A glimpse into His heart for us.

What if we looked at the doldrums as an opportunity? A chance to rejoice in the fact that He sees us as capable of handling the seasons with no answers. The times of silence. Imagine being on the high seas for weeks on end. Tossed this way and that as you face enormous waves that threaten to overturn your boat. Then suddenly, you find yourself in a place of complete and utter stillness. You literally can't go anywhere! While on the one hand you might be filled with worry trying to figure out how on earth you were going to get out of there, on the other hand, wouldn't there be a part of you that secretly relished the opportunity to just stop? If God's silences are actually His answers, we must learn to trust that they are His best for us in that moment. Maybe they are protecting us from some unforeseeable situation. Maybe they are preparing us for a new opportunity. Or maybe He just wants us to slow down. To stop and simply enjoy His silence. Right there in the doldrums.

Created from ingredients found at your local market, this French inspired dessert is easy to serve to company or family as a special New Year's Eve treat!

NEW YEAR'S EVE SEMI-HOMEMADE CROQUEMBOUCHE

INGREDIENTS

_ 40–50 frozen cream puffs, thawed

_ 1 cup granulated sugar

_ ¼ cup water

_ 2 Tbs. light corn syrup

INSTRUCTIONS

Place sugar in even layer on bottom of heavy saucepan. Combine water and corn syrup together. Pour over sugar and stir, just until sugar is wet. Heat sugar mixture over medium-high heat until it comes to a boil. Do not stir.

Allow to cook until it turns a light caramel color, watching closely as it can burn quite easily. Remove from heat.

Begin to assemble your pastry tower. Line pastries in a circle around edge of platter. Fill in the middle with more pastries.

Drizzle caramel, over top with a fork.

Continue to stack pastries into a cone shape, following each layer with a drizzle of caramel. You can also dip pastry in caramel to help them stick together.

Allow caramel to cool, until it forms strings with sugar when pulled with tines of fork. Using fork, begin to drape tower in threads of sugar until desired look is achieved. Serve immediately or refrigerate until ready to serve.

WHEN LIFE IS FOGGY

● ●

The fog had been lingering over the valley for what felt like an eternity. We woke up and fell asleep over and over to the same shade of gray on those cold winter days. When the fog first descended, I fully embraced the mystery of it. It felt romantic and spooky and maybe even a little bit dangerous. You didn't know what was just beyond that hill or around that corner. As I drove to school, the kids would play a game of trying to see who could spot the building first as its shadowy outline slowly emerged. The trees looked ghostly with their branches outstretched like arms reaching toward us. For a time, I loved the coziness of it all. It felt like the perfect excuse to have another cup of coffee and stay in my sweats for as long as possible. But then it stopped being so fun. I'm pretty sure that the moment it stopped being fun is the day when we found out that we were experiencing something known as a temperature inversion. Along the coastline and up into the mountains they were enjoying beautiful sunny days. But where we live, the inversion was causing the fog to linger over us, wrapping around the valley like a very cold, damp blanket.

By the time I heard about this inversion and the glorious sunshine others were experiencing, the fog no longer felt mysterious and romantic. It just felt oppressive. Why should they be getting sunshine when I could barely see ten feet in front of me? It got so that I was no longer certain if my mood reflected the weather or if the weather reflected my mood. I began to wonder if the fog would ever leave. When would I get to feel the warmth of the sun on my face? Should I find a way out of it? Get in my car and drive to wherever the weatherman reported a sunshine sighting? But my life was here in this fog. No matter how much I wanted to escape it, I had to go on living in the fog.

> Maybe the fog is actually where God does His best work on me. Because it's there, with everything else faded away, that I'm able to see Him more clearly.

I do not do well living in the foggy seasons of life. I want to know what's ahead of me and I really don't like change. My husband would probably say that is a gross understatement. And he would be right! In my relationship with God, this has been and continues to be one of my biggest struggles. There have been so many times when I felt like I had a big question mark hanging over my head, following me around wherever I go. So often, the circumstances of my life leave me longing to see what is around that corner or over that hill, and yet I find myself completely hemmed in by the clouds. So many times my life has felt foggy. I know in my head that there is sunshine just beyond it and yet, in my heart, all I feel is the awareness of my inability to get out of the fog. But in life there is so much that remains a mystery. There are times when we are oppressed. There are times when we don't get the answers we are longing for. There are times when we wonder if we will ever see clear skies again. And I believe that many times the fog is exactly where God wants me to be.

Is it enough for me to know that while I am in the fog, God is in control? Would I still trust Him even if I didn't know that there was sunshine elsewhere? Can I stay with Him here, in the fog? Second Corinthians 4:16–18 says,

> *So we do not lose heart. Though our outer self is wasting away, our inner self is being renewed day by day. For this light momentary affliction is preparing for us an eternal weight of glory beyond all comparison, as we look not to the things that are seen but to the things that are unseen. For the things that are seen are transient, but the things that are unseen are eternal.* (ESV)

I'd like to get to the point in my faith where I'm not always looking for the easiest way out of the fog. If I could begin to embrace the transient nature of the things in my life that are seen and look beyond them to the unseen, then perhaps I would be more willing to embrace the times when life feels foggy. My past experiences have actually shown me it is in the darkness that I feel the closest to the Lord. I call out to Him out of desperation and He meets me in that moment and offers me peace and comfort. And then I can look past the fog, past what is visible right in front of me, and see beyond it to the sunshine that I cannot see but that I know is there. Maybe the fog is actually where God does His best work on me. Because it's there, with everything else faded away, that I'm able to see Him more clearly. And see myself through His eyes. It's

as though I see myself sitting with Him in a field and all around us is fog but there, in that little space with just the two of us, just me and my God, there is sunshine.

There did finally come a day when the fog lifted. Granted, we traded it for rain. But there have also been pockets of sunshine. And with them comes the reminder that solid faith, trusting faith, doesn't shift according to the weather. It may be challenged by the storms of sorrow or send us soaring into the blue sky of happiness. But if we believe that the Lord is sovereign over it all, we have the assurance of His never-failing love. The kind of love that can break through any weather pattern.

THE ROBE

$\mathcal{J}$t was early in winter a few years ago when I realized that I was in desperate need of a great dress. I wanted a dress that could be my go-to for a variety of occasions. One that, with the right accessories, could be a little bit fancy, or with a jean jacket and boots could be perfect for a casual outing. I had recently read an article in a magazine where the expert stylist had informed me that a wrap dress would be the perfect solution. They said it would glide over my hips and show off my waist and was an absolute *essential for my wardrobe.* And, well, when you tell me something is *essential*, you had better believe I'm going to listen!

While perusing the racks at my favorite discount clothing store I struck gold! The *perfect* wrap dress! It was charcoal gray and oh, so soft. There were the ties at the waist that I just knew would do all the right accentuating. It was simple, yet elegant, and also seemed vaguely familiar which I took to mean it was definitely meant to be mine. With a long necklace, black leggings, and my black riding boots this definitely fit the *"essential"* qualification.

Sunday morning arrived and as always I was eager to trade my everyday wardrobe of sweats and a ponytail for something a little bit fancier. I cut the tags off my new dress, slid my feet into my black leather riding boots, and added a great necklace. I was ready. I walked through the lobby of our church just knowing that this wrap dress was ticking off all the boxes. Stylish? Yes! Sassy? Yes! Accentuating the positives? Yes! Yes! Yes! Yes! I'm pretty sure we sang the "Hallelujah Chorus" that morning during worship. Or maybe I just sang it to myself. Either way, this wrap dress was a home run.

> Perceptions change how we look at ourselves, which can be a dangerous thing if how we look at ourselves isn't grounded in truth, in reality.

I was still riding high on my wrap dress success after we got home. As I went to hang my new dress in the closet, something hanging on the back of the door caught my eye. It was so similar in color to my new wrap dress. It was also similar in texture. It had sort of bell-shaped sleeves and long ties around the waist and was oh, so soft and the hem hit right above my knee. And it was my robe. My soft charcoal-gray robe with ties that accentuate my waist and wrap around me just perfectly. My robe that I wear practically every single day. No wonder I liked my new wrap dress so much. No wonder it seemed so familiar. No wonder no one complimented me on my cute new wrap dress. It wasn't a dress at all. Oh no! I had purchased a robe that day at the discount store. A robe exactly like the one I already had at home. Holding them up next to each other only confirmed it. I had worn a robe to church.

After the shock wore off and I vowed never to tell a single soul about this, I tucked my new wrap dress/robe in the back of the closet where it belonged. Among the other shamed clothing items. I began mentally retracing my steps and wondering how this could have happened. I mean, that wrap dress was hanging in the clothing section of the store, not the undergarment/pajama/robe section. Then it dawned on me. It had simply been hung up in the wrong part of the store. I had *perceived* that it was a wrap dress because it was hanging among other dresses. I can assure you that if it had been hanging among the robes, I would never have thought to wear it to church! But it wasn't hanging among the robes, and so I assumed, I *perceived*, that it was a dress. I wanted it to be a wrap dress so it *was* a wrap dress.

It's so easy to be blinded by a perceived reality, isn't it? In our minds we make something the truth even if it isn't. We see beautiful homes in magazines and online and our *perception* is that everything in those people's lives must be beautiful. We scroll through Facebook and *perceive* things about each update. "They sure do have it all together!" "That mom is always doing so many amazing crafts with her kids. I'm sure she never wants to go hide from them in the bathroom." "That couple looks so happy together. I'm sure they never argue or struggle." We don't look at everything through "rose-colored glasses," do we? We look at them through *insecurity-colored glasses* or *judgmental-colored glasses* or *prideful-colored glasses*. But what if we were to put on glasses that were tinted to reflect the way God sees us? What if we were to trade perceptions for truth, not only as it applies to ourselves but also as we see those around us? Ephesians 2:10 says, "For we are God's handiwork, created in Christ Jesus to do good works, which God prepared in advance for us to do."

Perceptions change how we look at ourselves, which can be a dangerous thing if how we look at ourselves isn't grounded in truth, in reality. They might make you second-guess yourself, your parenting, your marriage, your friendships. They might make you feel like you need to redecorate your home even though you are struggling finan-cially. They might make you believe that if you don't have a weekly meal plan, you have failed as a wife and mother. They might make you think that some-times wanting to hide from your children in the bathroom is a bad thing. But when we are able to view ourselves and others the way He views us, we will only have His perception. And His perceptions always see the beauty first. Just like I saw the beauty in a robe that wanted to be a dress.

Your sweetheart will feel the glow of love with these personalized candles crafted from the heart.

FAUX-WOOD VALENTINE'S DAY CANDLES

SUPPLIES

_ flameless candles
_ woodgrain printed
 scrapbooking paper
 (found at craft stores)
_ metal word tags
 *(found at craft stores in
 scrapbooking section)*
_ jute twine
_ scissors
_ heart-shaped stencil or
 cookie cutter
_ Mod Podge craft glue
_ foam brush
_ ruler
_ brown Sharpie or paint pen
_ golf tee*

INSTRUCTIONS

Measure and cut each piece of wood paper to fit each size candle. Make sure to have the factory-cut edge at the top of the candle for a clean line.

FOR THE FIRST CANDLE: Trace and cut out a heart shape in the middle of the paper on the back using a stencil or cookie cutter. Using Mod Podge, apply glue to the paper and roll the candle, creating a nice smooth finish. Fold paper and seam and cut to fit with a slight overlap of edges. Apply Mod Podge to edges and overlap for a tight seal.

FOR SECOND CANDLE: Use same technique as above to apply wood paper. String one word tag into middle of long piece of twine. Knot at top of tag. Wrap twine around several times and knot and cut on back. String and knot second word tag and align slightly above first tag. Wrap around once or twice and knot and cut in back.

FOR THIRD CANDLE: Cut paper to fit. Lay out flat, and using a heart-shape cookie cutter or stencil, trace out a heart with a golf tee* (or something that will leave an impression in the wood). Add in initials and arrow. Trace this with brown Sharpie or paint pen (I used a copper paint pen). Allow to dry and apply paper using instructions above.

"NO" IS NOT
A BAD WORD

N o!" she shouted at me and then grinned. She was finally talking
and had discovered her new favorite word. I'm sure my reaction
didn't help, as I paused to look at her. How do they latch on to
this one word so quickly? "No, no, no!" she said with a scowl and then another
grin. She knew it was a game. A game where she felt free to express her one-year-
old opinion and I proceeded to express my parental authority over her. "Yes," I
replied as I shoveled in the peas, the airplane game having gone flying figuratively
out the window with her first "No!" After wiping my daughter's face and releasing her from her high chair prison, I started to work cleaning up the pea-covered
floor around where she had been seated. And as I worked I began thinking about
the word "no" and wondered when it became such a bad word. A word that I
myself seem to really struggle with. While my daughter seems to delight in using
the word, and using it loudly, I, on the other hand, find it to be one of the most
difficult words to utter.

For churchgoing women, finding the courage to say no when we are asked to serve is often incredibly difficult. And particularly in the busier seasons for a church community, like Christmas, we have made saying, "No, I'm sorry I can't take on one more thing, volunteer for one more thing, be 'guilted' into doing one more thing," the equivalent of displeasing God. But God is hungry for our hearts, not our works. We serve the Kingdom best when we have broken spirits for God's people, but not when we have broken bodies and minds because of weariness and fatigue. In Christendom, we often wear that fatigue and weariness like a badge of honor or a big *Y* embroidered on the front of our blouses. "I say yes to everything, see what I'm doing for God!" We have allowed the enemy to subtly whisper to us, *Your worth is in your doing, not your being.* We fall into the Martha Trap.

As Jesus and his disciples were on their way, he came to a village where a woman named Martha opened her home to him. She had a sister called Mary, who sat at the Lord's feet listening to what he said. But Martha was distracted by all the preparations that had to be made. She came to him and asked, "Lord, don't you care that my sister has left me to do the work by myself? Tell her to help me!"

"Martha, Martha," the Lord answered, "you are worried and upset about many things, but few things are needed—or indeed only one. Mary has chosen what is better, and it will not be taken away from her." (Luke 10:38–42)

We proudly proclaim to God, "See, Lord, look at all I am doing for You. I love You best because I arrived at church at 6:00 a.m. to fix the coffee, I greeted at the door before all three services, I volunteered in the nursery for two services, and the third one I helped clean the toilets in the preschool area. I know I didn't have a chance to spend time with You in worship today, but I love You best because I *do* for You."

I personally relate so much to Martha, doing, doing, doing for the Lord. But what about *being* for Him, like Mary was. Just being. Sitting at His feet in worshipful listening. Why does being still and quiet at His feet often bring about so much fear? Is it because He might tell us no? No to the hour-, minute-, second-filling activities that prevent us from truly spending time with Him? That He might ask us to say no? No to one more worthy cause or church activity or committee?

Is it something deeper than even that? Are we afraid that in our quiet we may be found out for what we really are? Sinners without all the answers. Women who, in reality, crave the approval of other people over God. Moms and wives trying to bind our families together with ropes of activities, good deeds, and a spot on the VBS planning committee instead of with prayer, faith, and trust in the Holy Spirit.

God wants you broken to His will, not broken because of exhaustion from taking on one more activity out of a false sense of guilt. A broken vessel full of holes cannot hold what God pours into you, and therefore cannot be poured into someone else. We are called to be a vessel, but a whole, healthy one so we can be ready to be used as He sees fit. "Therefore, if anyone cleanses himself from what is dishonorable, he will be a vessel for honorable use, set apart as holy, useful to the master of the house, ready for every good work" (2 Timothy 2:21 ESV).

> We are called to be a vessel, but a whole, healthy one so we can be ready to be used as He sees fit.

God will call you to His purposes, not man's purposes. He will gently remind you when to say yes and when to say no. Be slow to answer with a yes to every opportunity that comes your way, to every committee you are asked to serve on, or to every event you are cajoled to participate in; and quick to listen for the Lord's direction, even if it means we say no. For with every request you quickly answer yes to without seeking God's will first, you may be inadvertently saying no to something wonderful God has planned for your life. I'm choosing to stop viewing "no" as a bad word, but to see it instead as a word that can free me to be the vessel for God's purpose that He wants me to be.

ACKNOWLEDGMENTS

• •

FROM VANESSA

To Julie, Shauna, and Lauren: Never before has friendship been so clearly defined for me as it has since you amazing, godly, supportive, hilarious women came into my life. You are my kindred spirits, and I can't imagine going through this journey without you. I only hope and pray that I am for you what you are for me. And to all of my friends who have come alongside me and shared in the excitement of this book, thank you.

To my friends I've met through blogging, some of whom I've never met in person, I cherish the connections we've made and how we have all supported each other through the years. Thank you for dreaming the big dreams with us.

To Steve and Kathy, who raised the incredible man I have the privilege of calling my husband, thank you for your love, support, and encouragement in all of my endeavors. I'm so very blessed to have you both in my life.

To Ian and Lauren, my two most precious gifts, being your mom is the absolute greatest joy in my life. You challenge me, humble me, crack me up at least a hundred times a day, and teach me more about myself than I thought was possible. The Lord knew that I was meant to be yours and that you were meant to be mine. As I watch you grow, I'm constantly reminded of the great privilege it is to be your mom and how deep love can actually go. Thank you for providing me with endless stories and for not minding that I share them so publicly. I have no doubt that you will feel differently once you are teenagers.

To my Robb, without whom none of this would even be possible, your hard work and provision for our family has given me the freedom to pursue my dreams and I'm forever grateful. You lead our family with such grace and wisdom, and you are the best earthly representation to our kids of the love their heavenly Father has for them. You are the one who has seen it all, right down to the tears that flowed repeatedly when I didn't think I was up to the challenge of writing a book. Trying to sum up the depth of my love for you is virtually impossible. I am who I am today because of who you are. All those years ago, when we were first dating, my mom said these words: "Robb brings out the best in you. You are more 'you' when you're with him." And that is still true to this day. Thank you for believing in me even when I didn't believe in myself and for being such an amazing husband to me and the absolute best daddy in the world to our children. I love you.

FROM HEATHER

To my homeschool co-op moms, fellow bloggers, extended family and friends, both near and far, who followed At the Picket Fence faithfully from that very first post, thank you for being such loyal readers and encouragers of our work. There are too many to name, but each of you hold a special place in my heart!

To my dearest friend, Robin, you are a believer of me in all I do, and you are always there on the sideline cheering me on and being my biggest fan. We have journeyed many a mile through life together, down in the valleys and up on the mountain peaks, and through it all we have been by each other's side. I deeply cherish you and our friendship.

To my "in-loves," Bob and Arlene, thank you for loving me like your own daughter. Thank you for the gift of my "other half." I am so grateful you raised a boy into a man with such integrity and loyalty. We strive daily to show the same level of commitment to marriage and family that you have modeled for us. You are so very loved.

To Michael and Mekenzie, I marvel daily how your dad and I were so blessed to have been given the two of you to love and raise. We certainly did not deserve the gift of being your parents, but we thank God daily that He entrusted us with you. Being the kids of a blogger and an author isn't easy. You've never known when you were going to show up in the next blog post, or where your photos might pop up next, but you both have allowed me to share our lives with the world and have supported this little "blogging adventure" of mine from day one. I am so grateful for the young man and young woman you are becoming, and even though you are entering into adulthood, I will always see my little towheaded boy and girl when I look at you. You are loved from the very depths of my being . . . today and always.

To my Lee, as of this writing we have journeyed through life together for twenty-four years. The world says young marriage is doomed to failure, but we have proven that with God at the center, and with a daily commitment to put each other first, that marriage can last a lifetime. We have overcome a war and miles, and months, of separation as you have defended our country and protected it from harm. We have raised two beautiful human beings together, all while laughing and loving, and—let's be honest—sometimes arguing, our way through this life together. You are my rock, my constant. I am more deeply and passionately in love with you today than the day I said, "I do." I love you all there is . . . and more.

FROM BOTH OF US

Special thanks to our incredible agent, Blythe Daniel, who believed in us from the moment we met and who has become a cherished friend. And to the entire Worthy Publishing team, Pamela, Melissa, and Bart, who took our dream and brought it to life in the most beautiful way. We are so grateful to be working with people who want to honor the Lord and bring glory to Him in all they do.

ABOUT THE AUTHORS

VANESSA HUNT is the co-author of the popular lifestyle website At the Picket Fence. She writes and creates from her home in the Willamette Valley region of Oregon, which she shares with her husband and her son and daughter. Vanessa and her home have been featured in magazines such as *Better Homes and Gardens, Good Housekeeping,* and *Cottages & Bungalows,* as well as online at Country Living, HGTV, Redbook, Proverbs 31 Ministries, and {in}courage.

HEATHER PATTERSON is the co-author of the popular lifestyle website At the Picket Fence. She writes and creates from her southern home located in the suburbs of Atlanta. Heather shares her home with her husband, their college-aged son and teenaged daughter, as well as her two furry kids. Heather and her home have been featured in magazines such as *Better Homes and Gardens, Romantic Homes,* and *Cottages & Bungalows,* as well as online at BHG, HGTV, Proverbs 31 Ministries, and {in}courage. Heather's personal weight-loss story has also been featured in *People* magazine, as well as on *Good Morning America, Inside Edition, Extra!, Entertainment Tonight,* and *E! News.*

IF YOU ENJOYED THIS BOOK, WILL YOU CONSIDER SHARING THE MESSAGE WITH OTHERS?

Mention the book in a blog post or through Facebook, Twitter, Pinterest, or upload a picture through Instagram.

Recommend this book to those in your small group, book club, workplace, and classes.

Head over to facebook.com/worthypublishing, "LIKE" the page, and post a comment as to what you enjoyed the most.

Tweet "I recommend reading #LifeInSeason by @meetuatthefence // @worthypub"

Pick up a copy for someone you know who would be challenged and encouraged by this message.

Write a book review online.

Visit us at worthypublishing.com

twitter.com/worthypub

worthypub.tumblr.com

facebook.com/worthypublishing

pinterest.com/worthypub

instagram.com/worthypub

youtube.com/worthypublishing